KEEPING YOUR PERSONAL JOURNAL

KEEPING YOUR PERSONAL JOURNAL

by

George F. Simons

PAULIST PRESS
New York/Ramsey/Toronto

ACKNOWLEDGEMENTS

Excerpts from *Photoanalysis* by Robert U. Akeret, ©1973 by Dr. Robert U. Akeret, are reprinted by permission of David McKay Co., Inc. Portions of *His Affair* by Jo Fleming, copyright ©1976 by M. Evans and Company, Inc., are reprinted by permission of the publishers, M. Evans and Company, Inc., New York, N.Y. 10017. The excerpt from *A Sort of Life* by Graham Greene, ©1971 by Graham Greene, is reprinted by permission of Simon & Schuster, Inc. The six steps of keeping a "dream diary" originally appeared in *Glamour,* September 1975, copyright ©1975 by the Condé Nast Publications, Inc., and is reprinted by permission of the author, Norman Brown.

Library of Congress
Catalog Card Number: 77-99299

ISBN: 0-8091-2092-5

Published by Paulist Press
Editorial Office: 1865 Broadway, New York, N.Y. 10023
Business Office: 545 Island Road, Ramsey, N.J. 07446

Printed and bound in the
United States of America

CONTENTS

ACKNOWLEDGMENTS

Thanks are due to the editors of *Sisters Today* and *The Living Light* for permission to incorporate articles originally written for those journals into the text of this book. I am grateful to Dianne Zapotosky for typing a large part of this manuscript and to Marietta Starrie, who put this book in its final form.

I thank the many persons who in workshops, letters and interviews have contributed to the wisdom and "savvy" on journal keeping which is contained here. To them and to the countless others who wrestle with their lives through the written word this volume is dedicated.

Lastly I thank my father who taught me to try anything once, and my mother who insisted that I do it right. George and Genevieve have thus given me lots to write about.

INTRODUCTION

While countless people have kept journals and diaries and while quite a number of these have been published by their authors or by others who found them of interest, there is remarkably little literature on the process of journal keeping itself. What does exist is random and scattered. Creative writing textbooks spare a few paragraphs which encourage students to use a daybook or journal as a tool for learning, to observe life carefully and to write descriptively. Such a notebook is seen as raw material and serves as a pork barrel for stories, poems and other compositions. Anthropologists, social workers and ministry students are urged to write journals too. Recording encounters, interviews, events and their reactions to them is grist for the dissertation mill and the meat to be chewed in the course of clinical and pastoral reflection.

Most recently the journal has gained attention as a psychological and spiritual workbook. Though many counselors and therapists, gurus and directors of souls have recommended journal keeping to their clients and do use journal records in the process of working with them, Ira Progoff has been the individual most responsible for the development of the journal as a popular tool for personal growth. He and others trained by him have crisscrossed the country leading workshops in the dialog method. He has described the method fully in a book entitled *At A Journal Workshop*. Others have followed his lead. The Psychosynthesis movement emphasizes the use of the journal. Still, the literature remains sparse. I will review some of the available materials from these and other sources later in this book.

The variety of professional and personal journals is quite large indeed. Each approach has its own purpose and peculiarities which could contribute to the lore of journal keeping to the mutual enrichment of all. A comprehensive, in-depth study surveying the entire field of journal writing is desperately needed. The aim of this book, however, is far more modest. Its concern is to aid and instruct the individual who has chosen to set down in writing the mélange of events, feelings, inspirations, ideas which make up his or her life, and does it for some purpose variously described as understanding, growing, reflecting, praying, finding direction, knowing oneself, or sharing one's story.

There is a paradox here. Journal keeping has been such a rich experience for so many people precisely because of its personal, private, autonomous quality. It has existed for centuries without a guidebook. Part of me is tempted to leave well enough alone. But since I have chosen to meddle and to provide these guidelines and suggestions, I must preface them with the most important statement of this entire book: *When it comes to writing your journal, don't be concerned about doing it right. Don't worry about following the rules. The journal is your own book. It's impossible to go wrong.* Easier said than believed, of course. The approval and affirmation of others is probably the world's most sought after commodity. We yearn to be right with others at the same time that we desperately need to be ourselves. When the two fit together, it's heaven; in conflict, it's hell. Because the need to fit in with others is so very pervasive, it's important that there be such things as journals where the only thing that counts is to be oneself. To this task the present book of guidelines and suggestions is offered. Its only value is its usefulness to you. Let it be a servant, not a taskmaster.

This book, then, is written to fill an immediate need for information about personal journal keeping, ways of doing it and ways to profit from it. It is a need that I have heard expressed time and time again as I travel in the United States and abroad doing journal workshops. Journal writers, both veterans and neophytes, want to learn more about what they are doing or tempted to do. In these pages you will find a sharing of ideas, experiences and techniques.

While I feel that I am growing in my understanding of the journal keeping process and its uses, both from my own experience as a journal writer and from the abundant experiences that others have shared with me, this book makes no attempt to be the last word on a subject which evolves each time a new person sets pen to paper. It wants to be a useful collection of informative suggestions and processes, some of which I have developed myself and others which I have received from the wisdom and generosity of others. I hope, too, that it will stimulate more exchange on the subject so that even more helpful tools will be forthcoming. ·

Throughout this book actual examples and illustrations are taken from my own journal and journals of others. I take responsibility for the authorship of my own material. It is unsigned. Published sources are cited in the usual fashion. Excerpts from private sources are quoted with pseudonyms attached and are used with the explicit written permission of those who wrote them. In each case I asked persons who had been keeping journals for some time to share with me reflections on the process of journal writing, their joys, successes, difficulties, disap- pointments and failures with it. Wherever it was possible, and they were willing, I requested them to document these reflections by actual quotations from the journal. Most people were surprisingly willing to do so and mentioned that they would not even object to being named. For the sake of uniformity, however, I have stuck to my original promise of anonymity by using fictitious names for the writers of the excerpts.

PART I
JOURNAL KEEPING

CHAPTER 1 **WHAT IS A JOURNAL?**

Amid the incessant chattering of radio and television, the near instantaneous connections of Ma Bell and the anonymous intimacy of the C-B radio, thousands of Americans have quietly resumed the age-old practice of creating diaries and journals. Perhaps the greatest attraction of this return to writing is the opportunity it provides for being one's self away from besetting busyness and the demands and standards set forth by others. Helen Rezatto notes:

> No matter what I'm rhapsodizing or lecturing about, no one argues back, demands proof, or points out errors either in my logic or in my spelling . . .
> Within the sanctum of your diary you can be yourself—honestly; gay or miserable, noble or petty, soul-searching or superficial. Spouting off makes you feel better. If you have an image to maintain, you can forget it. A diary demands no poses. Nor must you apologize for leaving a blank space for a blah day.
> Dear Diary becomes your confidante, your confessor, your alter ego. Unless you have a snoopy family, no critic or censor need ever read your revelations— unless you wish it or are writing for posterity.[1]

Journal keeping is probably as ancient as writing, and is perhaps one of the reasons for its development; perhaps it pre-exists writing and begins with cave paintings or, as is the case with preliterate or illiterate people in the very carefully preserved stories handed on, at times verbatim, from one generation to the next.

Genesis notes that one of the prerogatives of Adam, when that mythical androgyne was set in the midst of God's word-made-zoo, was a nearly divine one. God had called the animals forth in creating them; Adam was to exercise authority over them at the start by giving them names. Perhaps only the dividing of Adam into male and female parts, their subsequent joining and the birth of new life struck our primitive mythmaking forbears (and if we allow it, ourselves) as having greater sacredness than the power of naming—language itself. How awesome must it have been when the first artists unveiled their works to their contemporaries. Did artists become the shamans and priests because they were able to capture that which was past or absent and make it present, by communicating in ways not known to all? Certainly we have primitive evidence that the shamans and priests and scribes had a powerful and sacred role as masters of icons and written words. The long forgotten artists who painted the Cave of Altimira hold us yet in their spell when we look at their work today.

Does it seem farfetched to travel into prehistoric times for the origins of the diaries of Anais Nin, Che Guevara, and Samuel Pepys or for the impulses which gave rise to Dag Hammarskjold's *Markings*? Not if we remember that we are dealing with an inclination which seems to go back to the dawn of consciousness and pertain to its essence—humanity's desire to contemplate or hand on in some fashion the important events, deeds, fantasies, dreams and hopes of people and therefore the need to record them.

Long before the trunk of human knowledge divided itself into branches of history, science, philosophy and religion, there was a need to remember and reflect on value-laden happenings and ideas. Today, when science has blossomed into a thousand disciplines, the same need exists to reintegrate deed and discovery into a meaningful panorama of life for communities and individuals.

The earliest journals were probably community records, created not unlike the "winter count" of the Plains Indians when tribal elders met at the campfire to decide which events of the season should be recorded in paintings on the walls of their tepees. A millennium ago and a continent away women were sewing a similar record, the Bayeaux Tapestry, which celebrated the Norman conquest of England. Before the advent of critical history the personality, judgements and tastes of the writers of public accounts were much in evidence. Such chronicles were often the stories of soldiers, explorers and spiritual journiers. Xenophon, Marco Polo and Aegiria come to mind.

Journals, logs, diaries and the like are still a part of such enterprises. Some are created by computers in the innards of space probes and airliners; others are still done meticulously by hand by anthropologists, social workers, writers, soldiers of fortune and revolutionaries.

It is difficult to pinpoint the emergence of the kind of journal which was meant for the primary or exclusive use of the writer's own self. Perhaps the emergence of history as a discipline and the passion for critical objectivity encouraged private writing to become a branch of its own where individual expression could run free.

When did the private diary come into being and for what reasons? While it may be impossible to answer this question in a historical sense without hairsplitting and verbose definitions, we can certainly come to some understanding of the original motivations by looking deeper into the reasons why individuals, in ever increasing numbers, keep diaries today.

As history serves the purpose of giving identity, meaning and value to tribes and peoples, so the private journal provides these same boons to the individual. Sheldon Kopp notes that:

> . . . the pilgrim learns through the telling of his own tale. Each man's identity is an emergent of the myths, rituals, and corporate legends of his culture, compounded with the epic of his own personal history. In either case it is the compelling power of the storytelling that distinguishes men from the beasts. The paradoxical interstice of power and vulnerability, which makes a man most human, rests on his knowing who he is right now, because he can remember who he has been, and because he knows who he hopes to become. All this comes of the wonder of his being able to tell his tale.[2]

Someone to Listen

Kopp goes on to say that in the telling of this story, there must be someone there to listen, and not only someone to listen but someone who cares. Are only they then to be blessed who have faith in a God or some personal transcendent or who have a friend or lover or who have found a guru or been able to afford a psychotherapist? Is "dear diary" just a poor substitute for any of these? A slightly more sophisticated way of talking to oneself?

Yes, there must be someone to listen, someone who cares even if we are totally alone. The ancient Christian theologians, with an astute understanding of the nature of the human person, and, perhaps not without wisdom, casting God in their own image and likeness, postulated that in the solitude of eternity even the Godhead talks to itself and listens and cares. So that the Godhead speaks, begets a Word and that the speaker and the word (unlike much of our speech which is only a pale reflection of our reality) are fully expressive of each other and stand in a bond of ethereal caring as powerful as the wind and as gentle as breathing. Those who have faith in a God of this sort are not without a caring listener. For they know that they too are a spoken word of this Godhead and a part of its story.

Speaking Our Own Word

Today, however, more people than ever live without this explicit faith or its functional equivalents in other traditions and cultures. While none of us can begin to live without others, maturity implies that we learn to listen to and care for ourselves. And so a trinity comes to exist in each of us as our organism speaks to itself, embraces its words and generates action. Unlike the image of the eternal God which may present itself to our minds like a gyroscopic perpetuum mobile, a dynamic stasis, our speaking and caring are generative and temporal. At the dawn of consciousness our organism speaks its own biological language. We cry for nursing and nourishment and we defecate on impulse. But then we are compelled to speak the social language of our race and the remainder of our life is a struggle to make it our own. It at once gives us access to others and contains us by its categories. Language shapes our minds and even our bodies. We speak our words and reinforce them with smiles, scowls, gesticulating hands and wriggling toes. At times we lie to speak our own truth and we dissimulate so that others cannot exercise a tyranny of words over us.

We need places to nurture and care for our own word. We do so in the warmth of our hearts and the privacy of our minds. Yet the word which is as real as our organic selves needs to be spoken aloud, to exist, to stand out, to be spoken to others. For both of these tasks the journal may be a step toward realization. It serves as a hidden hearth in which our inner words become malleable and capable of being forged into definite shapes that we can recognize as wrought by ourselves and as capable of transmission to others.

The journal is a word and a deed, a collection of words and deeds of a self in dialogue with itself seeking to articulate its inner word and to embrace it. In retrospect it is our story but in its best moments of making it is our very process and our being. The journal is a deed and only when it has been a deed many times over does the accumulation become a history.

Who Needs It?

After waxing so lyrical about the journal I may expect you to become skeptical—after all, is the journal really so important? What of the preliterate and illiterate? Can't we get along without writing to ourselves? Are we not innundated by paper, flooded by printed as well as spoken words? The journals of our race, its scriptures and its classics, are they not lost in the stacks of our libraries? Of the making of books there is no end; of the reading of books there is less and less. When our common story is now too big to be common, when we cannot any longer sit with our tribes-people and decide the winter count together to come to a consensus about which events of the year should be inscribed for posterity, when the survival of individual books seems more Darwinian than the survival of species, when who we are is impossible to extricate from the profusion of tapes and tomes, then perhaps more than ever before, we need to write a book of our own as we happen. Perhaps we also need family and community journals that reflect our being and acting and living together.

Certainly, some of the impetus for the personal journal must come from the fact that a tribal or national or community identity is no longer satisfactory or adequate for most of us. The acuteness of our yearning to belong is matched by the equal awareness of our not quite fitting in, by our mobility and the increasing tenuous nature of commitments.

It might be an easy step from here to damn the contemporary

world for its anonymity and lack of community or to accuse diarists of being misfits or narcissistic individuals, alienated and sick. While there are instances in which the charges are true, I choose not to focus primarily on sociological or psychological pathology, but on the individual quest for fulfillment which transcends the malaise of this or any other age and is reflected in the growth crises of every generation. It can be found in the *Soliloquies* of Augustine, the *Pensées* of Pascal, as well as in the *Diary of Anne Frank*.

Such writing happens in special moments and has movements and directions of its own. Not infrequently the journal is a place where tender new growth is privately and secretly nourished, away from the burning eyes and the blasting voices of others. It is the hidden chamber where awkward new steps can be practiced until we are sure enough of them to take them out into everyday life. Journals are often begun at life's turning points when one begins to veer away from the roles one has been identified with and thus begins to move counter to the expectations of most of those around us. Teenagers begin to tell their secrets to a diary in place of parents or peers. Adults turn to pen and paper in the crisis of middle age or when illness demands that a new or improved life style begin. Others write at retirement when the meaning of one's life must be secured and pondered. This is a time for memoirs and reflection, for assembling one's autobiography, a time for exploring old day-by-day accounts. Here, for example, is how one eminent author begins his autobiographical reflections:

And the motive for recording these scraps of the past? It is much the same motive that has made me a novelist: a desire to reduce the chaos of experience to some sort of order, and a hungry curiosity. We cannot love others, so the theologians teach, unless in some degree we can love ourselves, and curiosity too begins at home. There is a fashion today among many of my contemporaries to treat the events of their past with irony. It is a legitimate method of self-defense. 'Look how absurd I was when I was young' forestalls cruel criticism, but it falsifies history . . . Those emotions were real when we felt them. Why should we be more ashamed of them than of the

indifference of old age? I have tried, however unsuc-
cessfully, to live again the follies and sentimentalities
and exaggerations of the distant time and to feel them, as
I felt them then, without irony.[3]

Thus a journal is a daybook, a diurnal, a book of days, a book
of the single day which is my life. It is the ongoing book which
will be a continuing response to the nagging question, "Who am
I?" This inquiry is always at least in the background of my life. At
certain times it comes to the fore. In the morning when I am
young and anxious about what to make of my life; when in middle
age I wonder what is the meaning of my incessant striving—when
at the noonday of life I pause or am caused to halt and survey my
efforts and where they have led; at evening when the end of the
day is sure, when the sum of all is about to be added up, when a
new and more total perspective begins to emerge, and when I
wish to hand on something to my progeny. The journal records
the journey, the events and the distance traversed each day and in
the sum of days.

Are journals and autobiographies forays in the assault on
immortality? Consciously or unconsciously this motive can be at
work in much of our writing about ourselves. But how we carry
our stories into eternity is a much bigger matter than we have time
to deal with here, though it is not unrelated to how we carry on
and record our stories now. Not only the Judaeo-Christian sense
of divine judgement, but the *Jataka* tales of the Buddha and other
stories of reincarnation, and countless other ways of speaking of
"life after life" tie the story of our mortal existence to something
beyond death. Perhaps it is because deeds of significance, of
loving and valuing, ideas and intuitions, though caught in the web
of days and years, have already sipped the ambrosia of timeless-
ness at the banquet of the gods. What we know of eternity comes
from the vulnerability of time, from cracks in the present fabric of
the universe.

Productive Solitude
Diaries, fictional and factual, have been the companions of
the alone and the lonely. They have preserved the sanity of the
Crusoes and convicts actually isolated from human contact. They
have served as places of refreshment for those imprisoned by

social, sexual, economic and psychological barriers. Solitude is not without its benefits. As Merle Shane observes:

> Living alone is a life without mirrors, a life without a diary to read to see where you have been. And if at times it seems as if nothing has really happened, when it hasn't been recorded by another set of eyes, it is also true that when you stop relying on others to tell you what you see, you see for yourself and clearer still.[4]

To what she says, I would add, "Include a personal journal and the clarity with which you see can be even greater." The journal is an intermediary, a friend of a friend, capable of introducing us to ourselves as well as leading us up the road to where our neighbor lives. It is a letter of introduction from the deeper self to the everyday self and the record of their conversations with each other and the world of events and other people. Paradoxically our journals originate in a solitude without which they cannot exist and lead us to the conversations without which we cannot exist.

Stories of Oppression

It is not coincidental that oppressed minorities who begin to demand social change move quickly to telling their stories and writing their histories. Diaries both old and contemporary are called into service for the task. The memories of the aged and the struggles of the young become revolutionary scriptures.

Nor am I surprised to find that in recent times more women than men seem to have been and be diarists. Even the average diary for sale in a stationery store is fashioned in stereotypically feminine form and color. The oppressed talent and creativity of women, and their enforced private status have long been and continue to be conditions which prompt women to keep journals. These records mark the rising consciousness of women to the pain of their condition and provide stepping stones for their energies and impulses to be articulated in society. In attempting to answer the question of why women keep diaries, the editors of an anthology of diary excerpts responded.

> Dissatisfaction with the way love and work have been defined for the female is the unconscious impulse that

prompts many to pour out their feelings on paper and to acquire the habit of personal accounting on some more or less regular basis. The form has been an important outlet for women partly because it is an analogue to their lives; emotional, fragmentary, interrupted, modest, not to be taken seriously, private, restricted, daily, trivial, formless, concerned with self, as endless as their tasks. Confusion about the conflicting demands of love and work in relationship to the authentic self leads to loneliness, by far the most common emotion expressed in diaries . . .[5]

Perhaps there is something more to the journal which makes it curiously female. Patricia Hampl sums up this quality with the paradoxical note that journals belong to men of adventure as well.

. . . As Kate Millett and others pointed out, it is the root of an essentially female literary tradition with its cyclical (and circuitous) form, following the passage of time in its circle of years. It is also historically a woman's form, as letters are, as the kitchen is the woman's room. (But so saying I have to admit the other fact that was quite obvious as I stood in the midst of Jim Cummings' huge collection of journals. There is another group that can claim the journal as its traditional form: the army. Men, generals and privates alike, seem to be drawn to the diary form when they go out to kill and be killed. But maybe that's a good thing to remember. The point about the journal is not that it's a better form generically than the novel or epic which are often seen now as "male" or "linear." It won't, with the weight of its own inertia of "form," save anyone, or save a culture—female in this case—from the dark side of the human moon. But our attitude towards the form can make it, as Kate Millett suggests, one of the strong roots of a new culture. After all, the army isn't requiring new recruits to keep dream journals, but I know many women's groups who do this spontaneously).[6]

Initially—perhaps this is why so many teenagers in the hesitancies of adolescence have started journals—writing in this private book serves as an outlet, a place to say that which is not ready for communication to others, but at the same time needs to be wrestled with and expressed by the individual; it's like writing a letter to a totally trusted companion about matters that society or one's society will not accept. Emerging feelings, discoveries about the self, demands for dignity and recognition, joys and frustrations which are held back by real or imagined expectations of unbearable consequences begin to make their way into the written record where they get recognized and owned by the writer. The journal may be the first place where the individual clearly communicates to himself or herself needs and desires which are on the way to being communicated to others but are blocked by a lack of power, clarity or unspecified anxiety. This initial step in which one makes visible the inner self to the self, often reduces the fearsomeness of that which finds articulation in writing and becomes an effective prelude or rehearsal to actual communication with others. Having said it to myself and to my diary, I can now tell it to you.

Yet this privacy is not just a matter of defense. It has as Patricia Hampl notes, a positive dimension.

> . . . It is the lure of privacy that makes a journal so important.
>
> Privacy not only of specific thoughts or actions ("I don't want anybody to know that") but the simpler, more complete privacy of being alone, at least for part of the day, being alone just to see what will happen, what thoughts will come. It's the purest form of curiosity. I think even in times of stress or crisis the journal offers, through its privacy, a sense of inner freedom. This inner freedom becomes a habit, almost a reflex within the covers of the notebook.[7]

Building the Self

Because it can be reviewed from time to time, the journal has a stabilizing influence. Past experiences, feelings, inner and outer events and one's reactions to them are at hand to remind the individual of the realities as they actually occurred and were perceived. This does not prevent one from re-evaluating personal behavior and making new choices at a later time (it rather aids it since solid data about the previous behavior is there for the reading) but it sets limits on future portrayals of "the good old days." For the same reason it stands as a barrier to the deflection or devaluation of present experience (one admits it in recording it) and to the denial of past experience of its actuality or intensity (it confronts us in the record). Journal writing combats the distancing of experience by leading us in the direction of identity formation and self-acquisition and away from alienation and rootlessness and the mental health problems associated with anomie, the double bind in which one does not know where to turn for direction nor is it forthcoming from within. One comes to possess a self and a certain ambiance, a "home" in one's world of experience. The witness which the journal gives to life allows the individual to see that she or he has the right to be in this world, to take up space, to live without apology for living. One takes cognizance of one's environment and assumes responsibility for one's acts and feelings.

This same effect may be looked at in another way. By keeping a journal one is engaged in a process of individuation. The private sphere of the self is built up. The inner cohesion of the self starts to differentiate itself from others and from social stereotypes and where necessary stand in opposition to institutional and societal pressures. I feel my solidity and have a clearer sense of where others leave off and I begin. Individuals have repeatedly reported that journal keeping seems to have been an important factor in their ability to identify their own needs, to take stands on issues and to confront others. These are important gains both for individuals and for society. If one is tempted to look upon journal keeping as a narcissistic, introspective pastime, know that it is rarely that. My experience sees it much more as a workshop where personal effectiveness is fashioned, and this is at the heart of social interaction, politics and morality.

Meditation and Measurement

From a wholly different perspective, journal keeping has a meditative, ruminative quality about it. "It's a way of taking time out for myself." Persons swept away by vocational busyness, be they garage mechanics or assemblers, clergy or corporate executives, housewives or househusbands, find that their journals are portable sanctuaries. They're like the sudden cool quiet of the downtown cathedral that shoppers and office workers, both believers and agnostics, find to be such a restful relief from pushing, jostling and competition. That restlessness and insatiability which goes on in the factories, streets and commercial enterprises tends to possess our innards as well. We need resting places, demilitarized zones. Writing can be an emptying out, a laying to rest, a putting on the shelf, an unwinding which encourages both perspective and repose.

Writing and drawing as means of expression have their own speed so that the individual who engages in them is kinesthetically swept into another tempo. A slowing occurs and a new focus emerges. This may develop into an actual meditation on an object, event, person, act or feeling. I encourage people to write with as much specificity, color and detail as they can. In addition to keeping the record real rather than abstract and philosophical, it allows this sort of meditation to take place. Some people for whom this works well choose journal writing as a favored meditational discipline.

Finally, journal keeping precipitates change. Simply to record our behavior is to interfere with it. It is to see ourselves from a new promontory, to adjust our self-image and inevitably to give rise to new priorities in our habitual ways of acting. In this respect making entries in a journal is like taking snapshots and measurements of one's self. A photo album is a journal of sorts, and so is a weight watcher's tally sheet. Who and what we are is played back to us for pleasure or for pain (remember Dad showing your baby pictures to your teenage friends?). The emotional response triggered is a road sign pointing in the direction of growth. Unresolved situations are heightened (the teenager's embarrassment over baby pictures may be related to his or her emancipation struggle, concern with body image, etc.). Self-recording does several things. It gives us a quasi-outside perspective on ourselves and a way of communicating what is seen to others. The longitudinal perspective it provides is a way of testing whether what we are doing for ourselves (diet, study habits, personal-growth stratagem, etc.) really works or not. But beyond these beneficial effects, the native insight that self-recording changes people continues to be verified. The interference of measurement is valid not only for physics and chemistry, but in some analogous way it is true of human beings when they pause to perceive and describe themselves. Science knows that every measurement interferes with what it measures, so why not use measurement, self-recording, to produce change? Explicitation of inner psychic and spiritual needs and directions through journal keeping and related devices is an agency already at work toward their fulfillment or achievement. Self-recording, the picture of self generated by journal keeping, is an agent of change in its own right.

On Not Writing

Drawbacks to the individual journal keeping process are harder to get in touch with than the advantages. Not all people adapt to or enjoy journal writing. They just drop it and one hears very little about the reasons. The expenditure of time seems to be for some a deciding factor. Others whose flow of feeling and expression is regular and rhythmic don't seem to have a need for it. I have myself on a number of occasions been in retreats, workshops and intentional communities where the contact, support and communication was of such a high quality that the urge to write disappeared entirely. However, after such experiences in more everyday environments the need soon reasserted itself, and I also felt that I lost something in not keeping some record of those days. I have also come to the end of private retreats which included a review of my journal for the year and the use of writing as a technique for working at my own life, where I have felt "emptied out" in a *positive* sense. There was just nothing of consequence to write about, no unfinished business. I was relatively "up to date" with my life or had gone about as far as my capacity to work would allow. I had no need for it until later happenings would call it forth. This experience seems to underline the fact that the journal is a tool, not a master, and one of the drawbacks it shares with other ascetical tools is the possibility of our making it an end in itself.

A Time and a Place to Play

Much of the present interest in journal keeping has to do with growing. It is true that a journal is a place where growing can take place as well as be recorded. If what I have said so far in this chapter smacks too much of problems, therapy and "heavy" introspection, remember that the journal, being yours, can be whatever you wish to make of it, tool or toy. Even in terms of personal growth, it is good to be reminded by Gordon Tappan that,

> A journal is a time for play. Imagination in play allows more of the totality of what we are to come alive. When only somber and serious we tend to be stuffed into a tight bag which is our self concept. Play releases joyful movement. The imaginative play of an inner conversation, a dialogue, can allow the unacknowledged parts of the self to gain expression. What is missing in our self awareness we tend to project upon people and objects in our world. To begin to experience a projection as an aspect of the self, to own this part of the self, to free the energy locked in the projection—this is the major work of the journal.[8]

Despite the fact that we often speak of journal strategies and entries as journal "work," the essence of our best "work" is not drudgery but creative play. Somehow our wounds make drudgery out of things. That it is not meant to be so is the message of a variety of religious documents—the Torah, which assigns drudgery to Adam and Eve's Fall; the Wisdom literature, which pictures the spirit of God at play in creating the world; and, of course, the graceful image of that oriental "Lord of the Dance," the Shiva Natarajah, whose gyrating steps coax all things into being.

We can be so purpose-laden that we destroy ourselves even as we try to grow. We strive to let go of our striving and end up even more exhausted than before. So, in the midst of this panegyric for journal keeping and beyond the witness and the claims of others found here, remember that the journal is your own personal invitation to play.

CHAPTER 2   WHY PEOPLE KEEP JOURNALS

God Loves Stories

Elie Wiesel, a contemporary Jewish storyteller, begins his poignant novel, *The Gates of the Forest*, using an Hasidic tale as a sort of frontispiece. The concluding line of the story conveys the powerful message that God created people because God loves stories. The wonder of the story is motive enough for us also to attempt to capture it on paper. Language and literature return again and again to transcendent forms and metaphors to describe the force and meaning of human life. Whether our destinies are "writ in the stars" or in the hand of God or the gods, we note the stories of others, as well as those of ourselves, with awe and follow them with an insatiable curiosity. Beneath it all is the suspicion that our commonness reveals some truth, and by sharing what we know of ourselves, we are confirmed in the validity of our humanity though each of us writes or wants to write a unique script. One friend of mine who keeps a journal puts it this way,

> *I have always wondered (or marveled) at God being able to keep track of all the people and their lives and their stories. It boggles the mind. What is even more amazing that authors still find fresh plots, new twists to old—the same with music, from the same basic notes, the basic emotions, come so many new and fresh things. Maybe journal keeping could be compared to a recognition, recording and re-assembling of the basic notes, the basic theme.* (Anna)

My Romance with the Journal

Reading the diary of Anne Frank was one of the most touching experiences of my college years. It came into my hands as an unknown book in a French edition long before the English best seller appeared. I remember thinking as I paged through this teenager's diary with my analytic philosophy-major's mind that this was some fiction, a contrived piece; the sensitivity, perception and judgement contained there was just too precocious for so young a girl. The presumed fiction in places moved me to tears, and, when I later verified its authenticity, I felt both reverence and awe. François Mauriac had introduced the French edition and dedicated it to Elie Wiesel. Wiesel, only a name to me then, was on his way to becoming one of the greatest of the autobiographical witnesses of the Holocaust and one of my favorite storytellers.

After some years as a seminary student, I began the habit of keeping a diary of my own, not so much of events but mostly of my perceptions of my personal religious situation—things which did not get said elsewhere, prayers and laments and expectations. To this I later added, at the instigation of a spiritual director who had a natural instinct for behavior modification before it became a recognized type of therapy, some devices for relating my sexual instincts and other inner ups and downs to my environment and encounters. Journal keeping was a process which kept me emotionally and spiritually afloat in very stormy waters.

Several years ago, after a long lapse into professional busyness, I began journal keeping again, mostly out of a concern to figure out where I was going in life, a kind of star ship's log in which I hoped that the succession of ports visited by my experiences, feelings and thoughts might reveal my trajectory and aid my navigation. It worked so well that I recommended it to some of my student friends at Oberlin College and together we experimented, sharing from our journal entries and creating evocative techniques to help us explore our past and ongoing lives, with particular emphasis on our religious history and experiences. These first informal gatherings developed into a course entitled "Religious Awareness," which combined journal exercises and group interaction in the search for personal religion. It was an academically successful and personally exciting enterprise for many of us. The approaches and strategies which we created are available in published form under the title *Journal for Life*; the first volume is subtitled *Foundations*, and the second, *Theology from Experience*.[9] While we used these techniques for exploring the various dimensions of personal and social existence, the explicitly religious titles of these two brief workbooks "put off" many who could have profited from the methods.

This book is meant to remedy the situation by presenting a far more broadly based approach to journal keeping. I have not gone to the extreme of excluding explicit religion, like much of the human potential movement has done, for religion is, after all, a very real part of many people's experience and will find its way into their journals if they are true to life. Nor have I excluded theological or religious language in the presentation of the subject of journal keeping, for I find the wealth of such language in the religious literature, the scriptures and the myths of various traditions a rich source of alternatives to much of the techno-scientific jargon of our contemporary myths. I have made none of these so essential or doctrinnaire that they must be bought as they are. You may find other ways of saying and hearing these things. My own basic Judao-Christian bias is prevalent here, with a liberal sprinkling of things I have learned at the feet of other masters.

This has been a digression from the narrative of my own romance with journal keeping, but it fits here—journals are for digressions, and I assume that taking the same liberty in a book on the subject will prove the point. Actually, my story here begins to be intertwined with the stories of others as we look to them for testimony about why individuals actually do keep journals.

The Lure of the Personal Story

Perhaps Anne Frank was precocious, yet what is overwhelming about her story is the witness of inner personal experience which it contains. Though few may live in such dramatic circumstances as confinement in Nazi-occupied Holland, most people, teenagers and adults, are capable of recording their personal stories with their own beauty and poignancy. What they are willing to share of these stories provides precious clues to their present condition and their needs for growth.

Published journals and diaries, actual and fictional, abound on bookstore counters and library shelves. Curiosity impels us to climb into somebody else's skin, to see and feel both new and familiar things, as well as to discover others like ourselves, to go to forbidden places with mysterious strangers. Truth is not only stranger than fiction, it is more compelling.

The literature about journal keeping is surprisingly meagre. Individual journals have been reviewed and commented on from a literary standpoint, and psychological workbooks like those of Ira Progoff and the Psychosynthesis Movement have appeared with instructions on how to do them and some commentary on the process itself. Little has been said, however, about why journal keeping is a gratifying experience for many and has been an effective tool for the growth and maturation of people over the centuries. Outstanding personalities whose journals and autobiographies have been published sometimes give tantalizingly brief statements of the meaning and value of the writing process in their lives. Following this golden chain of personal experiences of writing could provide material for several doctoral dissertations.

Let's look at some of the reasons why people keep journals. In this chapter I will share with you not so much analysis or reasons, but will try to let people speak for themselves. With few exceptions this testimony comes from insights volunteered by persons who have kept journals in workshops, courses and personal consultations under my direction as well as from the experience of keeping my own journal. I have asked some practiced journal keepers to write to me about the experience. Some I have interviewed. In this chapter I have shied away from "notables," feeling that journal keeping belongs to a democracy we share, not to an aristocracy we look up to and emulate.

The Writers Speak

Some people are very explicit about why they keep journals. The simple desire to preserve memories is the most frequently cited reason for writing. As Helen Rezatto observes:

> That's why I keep a diary—because it all comes back—the details of those treasured experiences my brain would forget if I didn't have the magic passwords in my trusty diary to trigger my untrustworthy memory. Diary-keeping is memory-keeping.[10]

The loss of part of one's own story can be a motive for preserving what one can of it for one's own satisfaction and that of one's children. For example,

> *I am pregnant with my first child. I have decided to keep a journal of the things that happen to me and the feelings I experience. You see, my mother died before I ever had a chance to talk to her about what it was like to have a child and I was never able to learn about these things from her. I don't want my child to be deprived of these same things. The journal will keep my memory fresh and, if anything should happen to me, be a gift to my child.* (Hannah)

Many appreciate in some special way the gift of privacy which the journal bestows.

> *Why do I appreciate my journal? For one reason I am more open with myself here than in any other circumstance. I am not hemmed in by interpersonal dynamics as I am in talking with others and they with me. I will stutter less, choose fewer euphemisms, be less prone to dissimulate. On the other side, I don't have to put up with a confessor or a listener who will interrupt or worry about having the right answer, or go me one better, or tell me what I should feel instead of what I do feel.* (Charles)

Above all, the journal seems to be a place for feelings, for pouring them out, wrestling with them and learning to possess them as our own.

> *I find the greatest value of the journal for me is to give expression to my feelings. Lately I've been wondering if I make it into too much of a crutch and allow it to give me permission to indulge myself in feelings I would be better off to teach myself to suppress until they are no longer there. I have problems with that idea though be-*

cause I don't really think it's possible —most of what I read indicates that what I do not fully face in my feelings comes out in ways more destructive than if I permitted myself to accept whatever my feelings are and then decide how I want to act on them. But for a person who has been "head" oriented most of her life, I have some fear of the pendulum swinging too far in the other direction now that I've begun to believe it's OK to feel also —even when those feelings are not what others might consider "appropriate" (how I hate that word!) At any rate a good session of letting it all pour out onto the pages of my journal usually leaves me feeling more able to cope with whatever is bothering me. (Portia)

The feelings engendered by a relationship in crisis not infrequently provide the impetus for starting a journal. Often the recommendation of a friend or counselor initiates the process. In *His Affair*, Jo Fleming writes:

I suspect that for myself the most important event of these last years has been my writing. A new beginning of an unlived part of myself that exploded into life at a time of great stress. I think I learned the difference between empty pain and creative pain, without even realizing how lucky I was!

I suppose what has changed the most is what I do about feelings of frustration, how I live it. I experience my life more deeply; I have no rules or formulas to live by any more; I make no claims on myself or anyone else to make life easy or comfortable. What I seemed to have gained most of all is in my capacity to love and to be loved far more profoundly than ever before. And most of all I have discovered a quiet inner river in myself—a flow from my deepest being into words on paper. It is the last gift I expected from this adventure. I look ahead with neither dread nor joy; only with wonder at where I have been and curiosity about what lies ahead.[11]

She reports how her therapist prompted her to begin to record what was happening to her in her reactions to the knowledge of her husband's affair:

> . . . Eve suggests that since I have such strong feelings spilling out all over the place, it might make sense to keep a diary, pour out my feelings to myself—and then have the option later of showing it or not showing it to Jerry.[12]

One journal keeper remarked to me that she uses her journal to remember only good and pleasant things for fear that an inclination to make it a collection of troubles and woes would in rereading and retrospect be just one more cause and occasion for feeling down. While this is true for her at the moment, many longterm journal users attest to the opposite effect, namely that the rereading, far from depressing them is a source of encouragement. The memory of past dark days is testament to the individual's capacity to weather storms.

> *I made it through before. I can do it again!* (Scott)

> . . . Optimism in the midst of boredom and the blahs comes from past and present learnings, from the bountiful gift of journal-keeping which insures that mountains spring from valleys and that day follows night.[13]

Whether positive or negative in tone, pleasant or painful, the contents of the journal are invariable affirmations of one's substantiality.

> *I am reminded of the me that stood at so many of life's intersections. The recall of events, feelings and thoughts out of the past is a gift, sometimes a source of wonder as much as a source of satisfaction.* (Roberta)

For this reason I encourage those who find themselves collecting only certain kinds of experiences to experiment with recording other kinds of happenings and feelings if they can. It is a possible avenue to the appreciation of lost, forgotten or untried aspects of living.

For some persons, the journal seems to be a trouble shooter. It is a place to go to when things are going wrong, when a cloudy front of depression blows in, when the climate of relationships turns chilly or stormy. At such times the journal can be a disinterested party to talk to, an open space in which to clarify feelings, values and priorities.

A journal may begin on an impulse of hope or the recommendation of a friend or advisor. It continues only because it proves itself a trustworthy companion. For some the mirror it holds to life promotes growth by showing us where we are in the face of where we have been.

I was first introduced to the idea of journal writing by my daughter who started her journal in high school. She encouraged me to read parts of hers and realized from that what an excellent device it is for being able to keep in touch with where one is from time to time. (Portia)

One Woman's Story

Here is a fuller story of one individual's use of the journal. I quote it at length because it is a good example of the growth that can take place without any special method or process:

My journal keeping developed after I had written a lengthy account of my childhood experiences. In recording those experiences I was rather factual, e.g.:

"Through the mediation of the Red Cross my father, who was still living in Bielefeld, was informed of our arrival in West Germany. Because of the great insecurity and need of the time, my father did not want to abandon his job as a cook, rather he tried to supply us with food on his occasional visits. Unlike grandfather had predicted, my father showed no gray hair yet when we met him again, but both my parents were very tired, tired of homelessness, insecurity, fear. It took many years to overcome all of those acquired attitudes."

*I wrote this account in 1968. Through journal keep-
ing over the past eight years I realize that at that time I
idealized many things. The world of my imagination and
dreams, of what I wanted things to be or thought they
ought to be, was quite removed from reality. In 1968 I
described my home situation only in positive terms:*

*"In times of peace Marienburg presented a living
image of happiness and tranquility . . ."*

*"It was a happy atmosphere into which I was intro-
duced. Not only my parents but also my many aunts and
uncles carried me, literally and figuratively speaking, in
their arms, long after I could walk."*

*By 1970 I was recording somewhat more
realistically. I began to state negative feelings, but still
did not allow space to explore them.*

*"I had not seen them [relatives] since I was about
four years old. Obviously then one meets these people
almost like strangers. In a short time, my cousins, too,
had assembled. I got to know them a little through their
conversation but on the whole it was dead; perhaps it
was so since I couldn't work up my spirits after my thir-
teen hour journey . . . We stayed up late; I was annoyed
by the drinking, the type of jokes that were told, and the
noise that resulted as the drinking went on. I longed to
be alone. There was no chance for that—how many
people who live in crowded quarters have no room for
privacy?! Finally, around midnight someone suggested
we might go to bed . . ." 7/07/70*

*I believe that through my journal I recognized how
badly I actually felt about negative feelings. To me they
were not acceptable. Somehow I had a deeply ingrained
notion that to be sad, angry, frustrated, fearful would
make me unacceptable to other people. And yet, obviously, I did have strong negative feelings and when I*

*first started calling them by their names I was probably
amazed that the paper actually held still while I wrote
them down.*

*At the end of 1970 I met a priest whose teachings
and personality have affected my life very much. He
encouraged me to keep a journal on a regular basis and
to pay special attention to my feelings. And look at the
result!*

*"It was such a hard day struggling for hours with
resentment, anger, wounded pride, hurt. The question of
how I can establish friendships with everyone in the
community, of how I can be open and loving, looms
gigantic." 12/18/71*

*Not only have I learned to express my feelings on
paper, I can now admit them to myself and to others.
This admission had and has a freeing and healing effect;
to quote Martin Buber, "We can be redeemed only to the
extent to which we see ourselves." The journal truly
helps me to "see." I consider the journal a tool for getting in touch with my inner self, for raising ever more
searching and deeper questions, for raising my awareness and consciousness.*

*At times I have found that I can use the journal as a
process by which I can work through a confusing situation or bewildering feelings. I can start out with a set of
negative reactions and sort them out and work through
them until I arrive at a positive attitude or gain some
kind of positive value or insight.*

*"Tonight I felt so bad I would have liked to go away,
to hide in my room, to cry. I felt so angry and frustrated
and lonely and I thought nobody was aware or cared and
in all this inner turmoil and misery I felt very sad and
sorry for myself. It is true, . . . made very obvious attempts to communicate, but my unspoken response was,*

'it is too late; leave me alone.' I do communicate the leave-me-alone attitude to other people and so the very thing I want —understanding, compassion, kindness, love —is denied me. I should let others know how angry, sad, upset, lonely I feel; it would help me and it would help them to love me. Now I am only aware —my God, I still have to grow so much. But that is all right. Growth is life. Suffering leads to a deeper life, too —if it is conscious and positive. I want to, I really want to lead a meaningful life. I want to love, I want to be aware and spontaneous." 1/09/72

I have found that I feel especially drawn to writing when I am in pain. I suppose I feel instinctively that the pen helps me to work through a process of growth. My friend, whom I mentioned earlier, made me realize that in order to really grow we have to share with another human being, to be totally open and trusting, to be naked in the other person's presence. That requires a great deal of abandonment. I was able to let my friend read my journal and that was almost like an ultimate test of faith for me, but I feel that that, too, helped in my growth.

As far as problems in journal keeping are concerned, I have found that I am not always disciplined enough to write on a daily or any kind of regular basis. I believe that that could be helpful, too, because, I am sure, at times in the process of writing I might dig up things that I am not aware of on a conscious level. To keep a journal brings about a certain intensity of life and I do not always wish to be that intense.

I'll give you a few more examples from my journals; the quotes speak for themselves, pointing to the process of growth.

"Perhaps deep growth can only take place through pain. I have always found pain in my relationships with other people, especially people about whom I cared and loved. My relationship with . . . is becoming painful to

me for I would want it to be more lasting and more encompassing than it is at present. But I have to allow him freedom, too; but, basically, if anything at all is to come of our relationship, I will have to be honest with him—I want to be; I have nothing to lose." 9/24/74

". . . I am angry because he acts as if I am not important and what an idiot I am, for all I do is be Miss Pleasant and smile and show interest in him, correct his papers, mend his pants and plant him flowers. What an idiot I am!" 5/20/75 (I love this one! It truly shows how I have learned to admit my feelings and express them rather picturesquely. Incidentally, this is another plus for journal keeping, I enjoy reading my past journal entries. They are as fascinating to me as any bestseller!)

"Within my own short life span there are so many occurrences and many values that change rather quickly. What I considered of extreme importance no longer holds the same significance today." 6/23/76

"I mainly pick up the business of writing when I am in pain. Tonight I am not in great pain, just the recurring struggle in my relationship with . . . More deeply though it indicates unresolved questions. There will always be unresolved questions but I should do more probing." 12/03/76

In conclusion, I would like to say that I believe it is impossible to keep a journal and end up being dishonest with oneself, bored or disillusioned about life, sterile, hostile, dispassionate, because the process of journal keeping leads to facing life realistically. (Johanna)

Each journal keeper has a story to tell about the book which holds the fragments of his or her life. Most will tell you for the asking as did the few you have met in this chapter.

If you have come this far and are a journal keeper you have

probably begun to reflect on your own cultivation of this written account and what it has yielded for you. If you're wondering about whether to begin or resume the habit of writing, this might be a good moment to test the inclination. Pull out a pen and, if you don't have a journal book or diary, use some ordinary paper, and take ten or fifteen minutes to write down how you feel about journal keeping. What promises and problems do you feel it holds for you? What would be your expectations and fears? How does it feel to begin writing, even this little bit? Let this writing take you where it wants to. If you find yourself feeling anxious or blocked as you set pen to paper or come to a certain point in your writing, write about this feeling itself until it dissolves into something else. If, when you're done with this initial excursion, you feel like journal keeping is something you'd like to delve more deeply into, proceed to the next chapter for some very practical hints on following through.

CHAPTER 3   STARTING A JOURNAL

SELECTING A BOOK

Selecting the book that is to be my journal has always been a matter of some importance for me. I know many people whose journals are written on scraps of paper, school notebooks and the blank sides of sales pads and receipt books. Choose what suits you best. In choosing, however, here are some things you might want to consider.

Durability—If your journal will get hard use over a long period of time it will help to have a book that will not fall apart or lose pages easily. There are, of course, luxury editions, but a sound book large enough to last most people at least half a year is still available for five or six dollars.

Size—A small book is easier to carry, harder to write into. A larger book is difficult to tote but leaves lots of room for writing, drawing, pasting in and other extravagance. My own personal mean has been a book with pages roughly five by eight inches. It is large enough to open easily and lie flat, small enough to slip into a coat pocket or purse or to carry without discomfort. I also prefer an unlined, undated book. It leaves me freedom to write as much as I want and when I want, though I have to remember to date my entries. The unlined space encourages creativity and freedom of expression as I seek to move from the boundaries that I and others set upon myself in the past to an awareness of the potential of the present. On the other hand, some people have told me that boundaries such as lines and dates are very useful to them because they feel as if they lack useful parameters in much of their existence.

Flexibility—Does one choose a bound book or some sort of loose-leaf arrangement which allows the addition and removal of pages? There seem to be advantages and disadvantages to both. The loose-leaf format allows one to remove passages and set them side by side or to sort our certain categories of experience for inclusion in different sections. The Progoff method relies on this format and uses it very successfully.

I prefer the bound book. It preserves the chronological continuity of experience, which I find to be of the greatest value in the long term perspective. It encourages me to keep my mistakes as well as the parts of me that I am pleased with. I find it harder to rip a page from a bound book than from a notebook or loose-leaf binder. In this way I will have already begun to edit my editing.

The bound book does not permit the same kind of juxtaposition of related elements as the flexible arrangement. But this can be partially offset by use of a system of coding which will be described in Chapter 5.

Not all bound books are of satisfactory durability either. The best are sewn bound and capable of lying flat when opened and "broken in." It is harder to "repair" loose pages from bound books than loose-leaf ones.

I have yet to find a satisfactory loose-leaf format that is sturdy enough to preserve pages from accidental damage and loss without heroic efforts at maintenance. Linen or plastic-hinged pages, both lined and unlined are available at considerably more cost than ordinary loose-leaf notepaper. They are also bulkier. I have used them for a poetry journal in past years and find that they enhance the durability of a loose-leaf arrangement enormously.

One writer who preferred the loose-leaf style told me that she did it for the sake of privacy. She liked to keep her journal with her during the course of the day but also feared the higher risk of loss which resulted from toting it around. She solved this by adopting two moderate sized loose-leaf books, carrying one and leaving the other at home. She took with her only blank paper or at most several recent pages, and, after she wrote, transferred finished pages to the book at home. Here is her own description of the process:

> *I've never laid down any rules for myself so I write when I feel like it and sometimes I have missed recording very important events (such as a trip to Rome in 1974). I have included poems, newspaper/magazine*

*clippings and other such memorabilia that I didn't want
to lose and that had special meaning for me. I started
with a bound book because the impermanence of loose-
leaf didn't appeal to me. However, I have felt uncomfortable carrying my journal with me because increas-
ingly it contained feelings I was not willing to risk having
fall into unknown hands and I'm not the most careful
person with my possessions. The result was I'd write on
any scrap of paper wherever I was and then stick it in the
journal left safely at home which then became less easy to
carry because of loose papers. Another problem with that
was I couldn't always keep the inserts in the right place
chronologically so when it finally became too confused I
shifted to a loose-leaf notebook. Actually I have two
notebooks with rings spaced the same distance apart.
The sheets are 6" x 9½" and one notebook is small with
very lightweight covers and slips easily into my purse.
The other has enormous rings and a good heavy, hard
cover. I transfer to the permanent one any time I'm
leaving home and carry the little one with me always.
This has worked very well for me. It also makes possible
the use of the typewriter to write the journal when I'm
home which I appreciate because typing is so much a part
of me that my thoughts flow more readily via the keys
than the pen.* (Portia)

Not a few journal keepers prefer to type their entries or
transcribe them in typewritten form after they have been written.
In addition to those who prefer typing for its speed, some argue
for its legibility. Others see the original journal as a sort of raw
unfinished mess of jottings from which they select certain entries
to record or expand upon by typing them into a sort of finished
collection. I personally have a great love for the haphazard juxtaposition of odds and ends, writing and drawing which make up
my journal. For me the typewriter is a bit too mechanical and
impersonal—it robs me of some of myself. Therefore I have only
a few pages of typewritten material pasted in, usually writing
which was done when my journal was not at hand and which
proved to be too lengthy for me to want to copy it out longhand

directly into the book. Sometimes these typewritten sections are transcriptions of passages dictated into a tape recorder.

This raises the subject of tape recording. What about a voice journal? Certainly what we do with our voices carries a great deal of information about ourselves and our feelings. Electronic recording, audio and video both promise a lot as mirrors to ourselves. While I have found them useful at specific moments, in the overall picture I have not felt them to be as handy as the written journal. There are two basic problems. While one can record more quickly than one writes, playback takes longer than rereading. This plus the fact that one cannot visually spot entries makes retrieval and review of tape recordings a time consuming and difficult process.

WHAT WILL THE JOURNAL CONTAIN?

What goes into your journal has a lot to do with the purpose for which you keep a journal in the first place. Those who have kept professional journals or logs of one sort or another establish for themselves or choose a pre-existing set of criteria for selecting what is noteworthy and what is not. Sailors are concerned with winds and currents, tides and depth soundings; cultural anthropologists go rooting after customs and rituals.

The personal journal, however, does not ordinarily have such clean cut norms deciding its contents. True, we may use the journal to assess certain things, our weight, for example, or recurring feelings or actions. We may use it to chart our moods or measure our consumption of tobacco. Several such uses of the journal are suggested later in this book. Still it usually remains a potpourri of whims and interests.

Often journals are started not because we are certain about what we are looking for, but precisely because so much of life's meaning seems to be eluding us. We are filled with feeling and don't know what to do with it. Events puzzle us. Decisions are hard to make. And so we begin assembling the bits and scraps of our life which seem promising or problematic. Happenings, arguments with ourselves and others, the extraordinary and the too ordinary are scavanged and accumulate in this book with the hope that they will yield answers or point out directions for us.

Each person's journal will have a mood of its own—certain

predominant themes with variations and improvisations. Some will use the journal as a place to privately celebrate the wonder and loveliness of life. Others will pour out bitterness and disappointment. Still others will make it a record of dreams and fantasies, or a workshop for forging sense out of the raw material of daily experience. Some are books of inner searching and prayer. Dag Hammarskjold described his *Markings* as "a sort of white book concerning my negotiations with myself—and with God."

This chapter presents you with a panoply of suggestions about making entries in your journal. It is not intended to prescribe what to do with it, but, with the strategies suggested in this book, to be a rich source of suggestions to help you do what you may have already decided to do and to arm you with a variety of choices.

Certain suggestions are also made about "how" to write. These have a certain prescriptive quality—for example, the emphasis on being concrete and specific. These are drawn from my experience with journal writers in workshops and counseling, and respond to a malaise prevalent in our culture, a penchant for vagueness, for abstract rather than feelingful words. This in turn relates to the hesitancy we feel about making commitments and decisions. It is by no means limited to any one group of people, but does seem to increase with exposure to the educational system.

Here, then, are some of the more usual contents of the personal journal, ways of using the journal which many people have found rewarding and satisfying.

The Daily Account

In more leisurely times diarists described the details of the day with the meticulous attention of a Hawthorne novel. As an occasional essay in appreciation this is well worth doing. It will exercise our memory and expand our awareness. Whenever we capture the colors, tastes, smells and sounds of our experience, we make them accessible to ourselves at a later time.

> . . . *journal writing gives one the opportunity to really be right back where s/he was when the words were written. It reminds me of Penfield's study on memory mech-*

anisms which Harris translated into his "tape concept."
They spoke of a song, scent, or other stimulus triggering
an old "tape" wherein not only the memory (and some-
times even without the memory) but all the feelings sur-
rounding the memory are also with you again in a very
real sense and essentially you are back where and when
the tape was originally made. (Portia)

Such a record will be enormously enhanced if it tells inner events
along with the external details. The detailed diary of days spent in
a foreign culture may continue as a fascinating memory for years
to come; noting the fact that one had bacon and eggs or crunchy
granola for breakfast every morning at home will soon bore us
with journal keeping.

Usually our daily entries will be less complete and much
more selective. The events which stand out in our consciousness
at day's end do so because they are still important to us. These
ask to be recorded along with the inner events, the feelings,
judgments, fears and fantasies that accompanied them as well as
the reactions we have to them as we write.

I continue to insist upon the importance of trying to remain
specific and concrete, to use words that you can see and taste, to
use metaphors and analogies rather than abstract and philosophical language. Compare:

It was already warm when George came to see me. I was
surprised to see him wearing his down jacket buttoned
tightly. He looked like a big green frog in the puffy mate-
rial. I was disappointed and felt a tearful twinge of sad-
ness when he told me he wasn't feeling well since I had
been looking forward to spending the day hiking with
him in Columbus Park. When will we have a chance to
be together again, I wonder . . .

with:

George came around noon, overdressed and ill, so we
couldn't go out as planned.

If you are new to journal keeping and getting started with the daily record is a bit difficult, you might prompt yourself with some simple questions such as the following:

> If I could take a souvenir or a keepsake from today (or from the events since I last wrote in my journal) what would it be?
> Of the things which happened today, which would I really like to forget?
> If I were to pick a color to describe this day, what would it be? Write a paragraph about this.
> Make a list of people who entered your day in some fashion. Is there something that you would like to say to one of these persons that remained unsaid today? Write this, too.

It is the accumulation of such entries which provides the journal with its capacity to mirror our story back to us. It gives us, even if we do not do it on a regular daily basis, the kind of overarching perspective from which awareness, insights and decisions spring.

What does one do about the daily record on those days when it seems as if there's too much to write, when the day contained more than its share of significant events, when "all hell broke loose" and half a dozen encounters deserve notice, if not exploration, in the journal. This is as likely as not to be the day when it takes a superhuman effort to set pen to paper at all. When this happens, making notes is the most reasonable approach. Try to catch the essence of each situation in a very few but very articulate words so that you can return to them later. Allan, a friend of mine taught me a very workable way of doing this. Allan keeps a ferociously busy schedule as a consultant to management, hopscotching around the world. He has developed a system which he calls "headlining" to deal with recording overloaded days in his journal. Imagining that he is making headlines for the front page of a daily newspaper, Allan creates succinct and to the point statements about his day. He writes one-liners that grab both the essence of happenings and personal reactions to them. With such "headlines" he has strong memory clues which he can return to for further expansion. The very process of "headlining" is often a clarifying and consequently a relaxing activity which puts perspectives into the day's events and reduces the tensions of unfinished affairs.

The Journal as a Notebook or Scrapbook

For me the journal is also a place where I collect things that I fancy. Select photos of places I've been and people I love, headlines and quotations that somehow leapt directly into my heart from the pages on which I found them. I am especially fond of one liners, pieces of wit, wisdom and foolishness sometimes from written sources, but mostly spoken by friends and acquaintances over the years. I can't testify to their originality, but I do attach the names of those who spoke them to me, lasting credit to their creativity or, as the case may be, to their on-target plagiarism. Here are some of my favorites:

> *"Am I right or just getting older?" "Obviously both!"* (Exchange between R.R. and D.M.)

> *"Dialogin' with an institution's like pissin' onna tertel. It jist pulls in its head n' feet 'til it cain't hear nothin' comin' down no mo'. Then it jist moves out in the same direction it was goin' inna firs' place.* (W.C.)

> *"Luck is what happens when preparation meets opportunity."* (A campus bulletin board)

> *"Simplicity is the ability to see the world through the* ayes *of a child."* (My own)

> *"I don't know what I think 'til I've said it."* (M. McLuhan in an interview)

> *" 'I wish it would rain,' he said, 'that's one thing about California I can't forgive. It never really lets go and cries.' "* (A Ray Bradbury character)

> *"If you need a reason, one is as good as another."* (M.P.)

Occasionally in my journal you will find a fortune cookie slip, a horoscope, notes from people I have worked with and other odds and ends. I do have photos and memorabilia laying around my house in other places but a certain instinct tells me which ones are truly important and belong in my journal. The rest gradually disappear, are given away or retired or trashed when they outlive their welcome.

There is, of course, no reason why one cannot keep a photographic journal or even document one's life with matchbook covers. For me there is a line which separates my journal as a place where somehow my life is being worked out from the kind of items which seem to be pure whimsy or nostalgia. The line is not fine, but fuzzy. Things pass back and forth over it. You will establish your own sense about this.

Art in the Journal

You're an artist? Great! You're not an artist? Better still! The personal journal is a place where creativity can run wild, safe from the prying eyes and steel-trap judgment of critics. Drawings can often get at moods and feelings in the way that words can't.

I think that it is safe to assume that writing is the child of drawing, that pictures preceded pictographs, which in turn were forerunners of the phonetic alphabet which is the raw material of writing in the western world. This form of writing yields a certain kind of technological efficiency, linked as it is to sound rather than to images and ideas. This efficiency is not presented here as the climax of the evolutionary process, even though in the struggle for dominance among humans, it may be proving superior. At the same time that it seems to be triumphing, new visual media are proving the old adage that a picture is worth a thousand words, and, literate as we Americans are, we are reading less and watching more. The journal too, can be more than a repository for words, it can serve as the canvas upon which our images, dreams and symbols can be sketched and colored.

Just as I urge journal writers to search for vividness and concreteness, particularity and specificity wherever possible in their writing, so also I invite them to freedom of expression in sketching, drawing or just plain doodling.

My own only dissatisfaction with drawing is that I do too

little of it. I tend to resort to it only when I'm stuck or indulge myself the pleasure of leisure in a big way. Yet as I page through journal volumes, a number of sketches stand out as symbols of myself, particularly attempts I made to draw dream images when words could not convey the fantasy well enough.

Some journal keepers use an image, mood picture or mandala as a summary of their daily experience. Some do this exclusively, a reminder to the more verbose that everything does not have to be reduced to words to have meaning. Much of what we perceive is visual, and only a small part of that is the printed or painted word. For most people the written word, even when read silently, passes through a verbal-auditory stage on its way to meaning. Much of our thinking is done nonverbally, i.e. through the projection of fantasy possibilities, outcomes. We see our fears and hopes. We act out our stories on the mind's stage before chosing how to play our roles in "real life." The colors and sizes of things and the spaces between them all have significance for our plans and our feelings.

Letting the image flow onto paper no matter how poorly we draw is a way of getting a handle on some of these patterns of thought.

Letters in the Journal

Letters came into being when people who were too far away from each other needed to communicate. Wax tablets and potsherds preceeded paper and ink. Despite new and "more efficient" modes of communication, the letter has survived not only because it is capable of a certain personal quality but because of the authentic marks which one person can send to another. "See with what big letters I write to you," said Paul, the greatest of the Apostolic letter writers. Letters can be preserved and need nothing more than our eyes to come alive again.

Great physical distance is not the only form of separation which can be bridged by writing. Lovers leave little notes for each other, like surprise kisses, to bridge the time of their brief separations. What cannot be said for fear or excess of feeling finds its way in an envelope.

It is certainly possible to hide behind letters as well as to reveal one's self through them, but that is another issue entirely.

Later we will talk about the use of the letter as a kind of basic strategy for journal work. Here we are concerned with keeping actual letters one sends and receives in the journal. There is no doubt that personal correspondence can provide additional keys to self understanding. Bundles of letters kept for nostalgia's sake have on later perusal opened doors to personal insight and unlocked snafud relationships. They, like journals whose privacy is violated, can be a load of trouble, too.

For awhile it seemed as if the personal letter was a dying form of expression. Putting it in writing continued to be de rigueur for business, bills and members of Congress, but we turned to the telephone to speak to spouses, lovers, faraway friends and relatives. Recently, despite the cost of stamps, there seems to have been a rediscovery of the particular power of the letter (which it shares with the journal) of using silence and privacy to penetrate more deeply and express more succinctly what it is we have to communicate to each other. Letter writing is becoming more popular again.

What about using the journal as a collecting place for letters? It is easier to keep the letters we receive than the ones we send. Making copies of personal correspondence, especially for one who writes rather than types, is a cumbersome and messy process. Occasional letters of importance might be copied into the journal before being sent. If, however one maintains a large correspondence, this becomes too difficult and time consuming. Carbons and xerox machines can give us paste-in copies.

There is wisdom and advantage to being able to see one's correspondence in the context of the other things going on in one's life as recorded in the journal, and the letter may include details which we might not otherwise note. For me, the willingness to include a letter in my journal is a test of the honesty and sincerity with which I have written to the other. Sometimes the actual letters get revised when I find myself unwilling to own them enough to put them in my journal for keeps.

Dreams

One of the most significant discoveries of modern humankind has been out penetration of layers of personality which lie below the conscious mind. Indeed we have learned that this conscious weighing, planning, classifying, judging, organizing mind of ours is only one function, albeit a crucially important one, of our personality. While this mind gives us great power to manage our world, to manipulate and use its elements, divorced from our other functions of sense and understanding, from fantasy and feeling, it can destroy us and deprive us of our dearest needs and fulfillments personally, and, collectively, fashion an inhuman society. In the journal there will be space to let usually fettered parts of the self emerge. There will be space to play and to pray, to fantasize and make believe, as well as to record facts and events. Dreams, daydreams and fantasies are the most common incursions on the nonrational side of our personalities. They are ready material for our writing and reflection.

The journal serves both as the repository and the workbook for our dreams. This section will serve as a brief introduction to the uses of the journal for dreaming. I choose to keep it short—just enough for beginners to work with—for two reasons. First, the study and interpretation of dreams is an ancient as well as a contemporary concern, a study in its own right. Secondly, there is already a vast literature on the subject, religious, mystical and esoteric, as well as a blooming scientific study of the physiology and psychology of dreaming. I could do no better than recommend to persons wishing to delve deeper into this matter the excellent, no-nonsense approaches taken by Ann Faraday in her two books *Dream Power* and *The Dream Game*.[14] She provides more information than most individuals will need for several years of exploring the dream dimension of their lives.

There are dream interpretation books galore, psychotherapeutic discussions as well as dictionaries of images and symbols from religious and occult sources. I would recommend in general that beginners stay away from these last for several reasons. I feel that it is important for each person to establish contact with his or her own awareness of dreaming and the innate sense that this brings with it. Furthermore, many of these books give the impression that one interprets dreams as one naively translates a foreign language, looking up each individual word in a dictionary. While one who does not know the language might possible make some sense out of a French text, for example, by doing this, the odds of getting the message correctly are pretty poor and there is a high probability of a serious misunderstanding. Moreover, even though there seem to be certain common and even archetypal symbols spoken by our dreams, dreaming is a far more personal language than English or German. Its words are made up day by day, and the feeling tone, like the inflection of the spoken word, is as important as the symbols used.

Dreams do not have to be "translated," understood or interpreted word for symbol to be useful. Most dreams are lost to us entirely, played out beneath the level of consciousness in the theater of sleep. Here they work their magic of renewal anonymously. How often issues are resolved when we "sleep on them."

The importance of recalling dreams seems to be related to finishing them, bringing them to their needed resolution. While some seem to work their resolution with no awareness whatever on our part, others are only remembered as fragments, or we remember that we dreamt, but not what. For some we have vivid, very complete but puzzling stories. I wonder if when we bring a dream into the waking state, it is not often because its resolution is interrupted; i.e., the unconscious lacks the resources to complete what must be done and the conscious person must take over? It could also be true that when we do not recall some dreams we do not need them.

Our approach to exploring dreams with the journal will be twofold, experiencing the dream and then carrying it forward to resolution. In certain instances, feeling one's way through the dream will be all that is needed for the substance of its message to be apprehended. At other times one must extend it by associations, dialogues, story-telling, or fantasy. Right now we are only concerned with beginning the process of dream exploration by getting a good, useful record of the dream itself.

The first step, of course, is entering the dream in your journal. Keep your pen and journal close at hand when you retire so that you will have it readily available when waking from a dream. Time spent fumbling for writing materials will cause you to lose some of the delicate memory traces which hold your dream story together. You can also use a readied tape recorder and transcribe the dream later into your book.

Write or record the dream in the present tense, just as if it's actually taking place. Make the account as graphic and complete as possible, paying attention to the feelings as well as details and action. Jot down anything else that comes to mind along with or as a consequence of the dream or any associations which suggest themselves.

Be prepared to record more than one dream in a night. Dreams tend to be related and to build on each other. Those which occur "back to back" often help to elucidate each other.

Waking fantasies which haphazardly occur can be recorded in the same fashion as dreams. Information is given in the next chapter on what to do with dreams and fantasies after they have been captured in your journal.

If dreaming and fantasy are somehow difficult for you, begin writing your feelings and thoughts about them. This may loosen some of the obstacles to their flow.

Fantasies and Meditations

Fantasies which simply occur to the waking mind can be recorded and worked with in much the same fashion as dreams. Usually their language is not as difficult to fathom since the mind exercises some influence on the logic and content of the imagination.

Alongside the fantasies, the daydreams which just "happen" in the normal course of our awareness, it is also possible for us to deliberately enter into the fantasizing process, setting off on fantasy journeys, meditating or simply observing our stream of consciousness.

It is possible to go about this at various levels of awareness from simple quiet attention to deep, even trance-like concentration. There are many approaches to creative fantasy and meditation. Most suggest that we put ourselves physically and emotionally in an alert but relaxed state. Deep breathing and some stretching exercises can ready our bodies. Assuming a comfortable but not sleep-inducing posture will help. Taking pen in hand and recording the flow of images or the sequence of a fantasy is a powerful adjunct to this process. Writing gives a point of focus and concentration so it is possible to be even more absorbed in what takes place.

While Ira Progoff recommends writing at the very time that one is immersed in unconscious exploration or fantasy, others choose to fantasize first and record later. (This is also a place where the tape recorder could be a happy adjunct to journal work.) Here is Kathleen Cox's description of how she goes about it.

> . . . We have a comfortable old gold chair with a high back in our livingroom. In the morning, after my husband and children have left for the day, I sit in that chair, close my eyes, and start listening to my breathing. I have found this empties my head—it is impossible for me to think while concentrating on my breathing. After a time, I visualize myself descending into darkness, being completely surrounded by darkness. At this stage, I am no longer concentrating on my breathing. Instead, I am concentrating on the images which float up out of the darkness. I choose which one to follow and a scene or a small play unfolds before my inner eye. When I come out of it, I go into my study and write down as simply as possible what I have seen. I have tried very hard to be true to the vision, not to manipulate in any way this gift which has brought me so much inner strength and which has helped in an immeasurable way to make me whole.[15]

The record of our fantasy life may then be compared with our active factual existence recorded in the other parts of the journal for coherence or dissonance, reinforcing our development or pointing to tasks of integration that lie before us. Having this record allows us to build on it by further writing and to explore it by use of some of the basic strategies.

WHEN DOES ONE WRITE IN THE JOURNAL?

"When?" in this case is a two part question. On one hand it refers to such very practical questions "At what time time of day do I write?," "How often?" or "In what circumstances?," e.g., solitude or streetcars—the two are not contraries. On the other hand it raises the more sensitive issues represented by questions like "Do I write in painful moments or happy ones?" or "Is it good to write when I am depressed?" Let's look at the more practical questions first.

The journal, like any other personal growth tool or spiritual discipline is meant to be a servant, not a master. It exists to disencumber us of our excess baggage of worries, fears, and guilt, not to burden us with an additional load. The joys, sorrows and memories we write about will hopefully be carried like helium-filled balloons, lightening the rest, not adding to it.

Like any process it will require a certain amount of exploratory immersion and fidelity to be productive. One needs to trust it a bit. To make it a duty, however, and to feel guilty about negligence is putting the cart before the horse and the surest way to calling it quits in a hurry.

Many persons begin journal keeping on their own almost spontaneously, triggered at most by some mood, incident or accidental circumstance, the gift of a diary, depression after the birth of a child or death of an intimate, a vacation travelog, hearing or reading of someone else's diary or journal keeping. From this modest start there may evolve many years of journal keeping, sometimes a lifetime. There may be interruptions of weeks, months or years, yet the flow continues.

Some people try often and fail and only really become devotees after the apprenticeship of a course, retreat or workshop which deeply immerses them in the journal process to the point where they realize some of its actual benefits for themselves. I have found strategies like those contained in the second part of this book to be very valuable for beginners and veterans alike. As introductory tools they yield new and surprising perspectives from which to view one's self. They will benefit inveterate journal keepers at times when impasses occur and as an enrichment to everyday writing. In a short period of time they model some of the results which one can derive from keeping a journal. The purpose of this book and especially of the inclusion of the strategies is to alleviate the initial confusion felt by many first time journal keepers as well as to enhance the work of those long at it.

Some times in life seem more conducive to writing than others. Journals are not everyone's cup of tea. If having tried writing, you don't like it or it doesn't work for you, hurrah—life has something else in store for you, other ways of enjoying your riches, solving your problems and growing into who you will be.

Some people choose to set aside a certain time of day or

week to attend to their journals. Beginners might try to do this for a while, not as an inflexible rule, but simply to create time and place in their lives for a new dimension of reflection. Work, occupation and other preoccupations have a way of expanding to fill all available time. Journal keeping as a fledgling reflective practice runs the risk of getting nosed out of the nest by other species of concerns long before it is able to fly on its own. Some initial protectiveness will nourish its growth into a strong ally.

While I began a diary in this way many years ago, I have long ceased to write with any pattern of regularity. I may make as many as six or seven entries in a single day, some individual entries being five or six closely written pages long. Occasionally as much as three weeks may pass without an entry or even a remembered dream. Usually there are small and large entries occurring every day or every several days.

Certain elements will affect the frequency of my writing. One of these is other writing. Since part of my profession is that of writer, intense concentration in that area may leave me particularly drained of things that I want to say or the energy to say them. Group work and counseling which form another dimension of my work find me processing and finishing a lot more of my personal concerns as they happen. There is not much stored up for the journal. Letter writing has a like effect. Expressing myself in writing to close friends and intimates leaves me disinclined to repeat the same things in my journal. In sum, the frequency of journal entries seems best when it becomes an organic response, though it may begin as or be protected by making it a programmed activity.

Individuals who find it possible and desirable to have their journal available to them most of the time either carry it with them or keep it at hand where they spend the best part of their day. Then it can be used at planned or odd moments during the day, whenever one feels like it.

Others choose to use the journal as a midday pause and/or as a way of concluding the day before retiring. Thus the journal comes to rest on the nightstand where it lies ready to receive the wandering dreams which are remembered upon waking.

While I tend to use my journal whenever the inclination strikes me and the book is at hand—really pressing things get written on scraps of paper even when the journal is not around, only to be copied or pasted in later—I have found the evening hours and the moments before retiring to be the most natural times for turning to my journal. Then, the busyness of the day has a chance to fall into place as I write about both the satisfaction of things finished and the uncertainty of those still pending. Not infrequently this review of the day ends with my falling asleep, pen in hand. The review relieves the tension of the day and allows tiredness to follow its course. When I discovered this, it led to my personal prescription of journal keeping as an effective cure for insomnia. At least that kind of sleeplessness which is rooted in an overstimulated mind, in the whirling of concerns which will not shut down, can be dealt with by setting them out on the pages of a book which can be neatly closed. There they will keep until another day and we, having entrusted them to the journal, can close our eyes and take from sleep and dreaming the strength we need to confront them later on. Try the journal before getting hooked on sedatives and tranquilizers or martinis.

This is not unlike the traditional night prayer of Western monks who examined the concerns of their hearts and comménded their spirits to God in the office of Compline at the close of each day. People who use a journal as an explicit part of their religious life will often find that the journal still fits well into this kind of prayer.

Perhaps it goes without saying that the environments which individuals choose for specific activities such as journal keeping are largely a matter of personal taste and "to each his or her own" is the watchword. Some look for absolute solitude and quiet; others are able to make space for themselves and to venture inward even in crowded and noisy circumstances. Any comment I make here is just an underline to horse sense. If you demand perfect conditions you will find yourself doing precious little writing; if you cannot muster some uninterrupted time you will probably not go very deep.

Sometimes creating a mood of stillness and awareness makes writing possible; at other times beginning to write changes us and creates its own mood. I find that my daily entries are made in a variety of circumstances, some rushed and some relaxed. More serious reviews require more protected circumstances to be fruitful.

The second kind of "when" question that I mentioned at the

head of this chapter had to do with the right moment for myself to write. Obviously one should not go looking for a special mood before one can write. *De facto*, individuals do find themselves more prone to write when they are feeling a certain way, depressed for example, than when they are feeling differently, excited for example.

Being conscious of when one is inclined to write may be a clue about one's life and priorities far beyond journal keeping. More about this later. If one does notice that writing only occurs in certain moods, a conscious effort might be made to write at other times. This might signal a breakthrough into a new self-awarenesss. If not it may mean that the journal is serving the individual in an adequate manner already.

ONE JOURNAL OR MANY?

A strange sounding question? Perhaps. However I do know quite a number of people who work with several books at one time in their journal keeping. Some have separate books for recording dreams. One has a "body book" that contains everything pertaining to physical well-being. Some keep personal journals alongside professional ones, or books that they are willing to share from alongside ones that are strictly private.

Though I advise individuals to move in the direction of having one book which is the journal, there may be times and situations when more than one is called for, when keeping one book would clutter it with so much extraneous data as to confuse its purpose. Since I for example attend frequent lectures and conferences and read many books, I find it necessary to keep the notes that I take on these in a separate place. Things of personal significance will find their way into the journal but the inclusion of all my reports and running observations would make my journal so voluminous that my personal statements and concerns would be lost in the rest. Those who do much less of this might be quite comfortable with taking notes and digesting what they read and hear directly in the pages of their journals. I will sometimes read a book very slowly and reflect on it in my journal piece by piece sometimes writing just as much as or more than I read.

Doris Lessing (*The Golden Notebook*) recounts her passage from a variety of notebooks to a single journal as a process of integration in her life as well as her writing. If in the process of writing you find a number of compartments asserting themselves, the effort to integrate them in a single journal might provide you with some clues as to whether and how they fit together for you.

PRIVACY

Privacy is a large practical issue. The horror of having one's journal fall into the "the wrong hands" is a real deterrent to journal keeping for many people. A privacy issue can exist between teenagers and parents, companions and lovers and mates, members of intentional communities and communes. Authentic journal keeping requires as much security around the issue of privacy as the individual needs to enable her or him to write about whatever is important. Part of the need for privacy diminishes along with our fears as we grow confident of our place in the world and more open and direct with others, but it never entirely disappears. I urge individuals to be realistic about this. On the other hand, it is encouraging to note that our public concern for and moral sense of the protection of the privacy of individuals has been growing in the United States. It is evident both in our reaction to governmental debacles and in the way I see individuals giving others "space" in families and other relationships. Some religious groups still demand access to this privacy, but the individual's choice to join or remain in such groups tends more and more to be voluntary.

I have met housewives who are afraid to write about what they feel for fear their children will pry into it. I know South Americans who hesitate to write anything personal for fear of the police. Individuals in difficult circumstances will decide whether to write at all. The journals of the persecuted are among some of our greatest human documents. Yet they have often been used for torture, intimidation and entrapment.

Persons without privacy or those for whom the fear of privacy is so great that it prevents them from writing might consider still doing those things which require privacy but destroying them when they are done with them. This sacrifices the benefits of perspective and longrange review, but does allow the experience of self-expression and the comprehension which often occurs in the writing and immediate reading of the entries.

Dialogue House, the agency of the Intensive Journal according to the Progoff method, provides a registry service for its members. Each journal is given a number along with the Dialogue House address and the promise of a reward to the finder. In this way a lost book will be returned to the owner without its being marked with the writer's name and address. Those who have anxiety about the loss or theft of the journal might establish some trusted friend or neutral mediator for its anonymous return. For some a simple Post Office Box number would be adequate.

The journal brings into focus and calls us to wrestle with that lack of trust which is at the root of so many personal and political ills. It is a way of coming to trust ourselves and building that trust into larger situations of which we are a part.

More will be said about privacy in the section which deals with special applications of the journal process to groups and education in Chapter 5.

CHAPTER 4   THE JOURNAL REVISITED

Making entries in a journal is like digging a garden. Just turning the soil may reveal a treasure which lies close to the surface. When it comes to our daily accounts, however, writing is like planting a package of mixed seeds. Some of what we sow will spring up almost immediately; other fruits and flowers will emerge at odd seasons to nourish and grace our lives when we need them most. Certain entries are annuals, others perennials. Some have a one-time value; others appear again and again to enrich us. A few may lie dormant for years before germinating. Some do not grow at all.

This chapter has to do with how one cultivates, waters, fertilizes and harvests this very mixed garden. What is the value of the journal once it is written? What can one do to get more meaning out of entries one has made? Besides the variety of personal and professional uses made of the journal and the fact that journals may become family treasures, historians' delights, or boons to biographers, what further benefits can the writer derive from his or her own work? What are the immediate and long term possibilities for enrichment? What does one do with journal entries once they are written? As the days add up to months and years and the collected diaries begin to keep each other company in a drawer or on a bookshelf, can we continue to learn and grow from them? This section will concern itself with these questions.

I have already alluded to the fact that the very act of writing in the journal, the outward expression and actualization of the as yet unformed inner impulses and thoughts of the individual, can be a significant part, perhaps the chief part, of its value to the author. This is especially true of those entries which have to do with our feelings, with personal decisions and interpersonal struggles.

THE FARTHER REACHES OF JOURNAL KEEPING

Much of the profit of journal keeping is gained in the moments when it is being done. The movement from concept and feeling to conscious articulation in writing, from inner germ to outer expression—the ability that this gives us to immediately speak and survey ourselves—is probably for most people the most attractive feature and compelling motivation for journal keeping.

Often the speaking is separated somewhat in time from the survey. Entries made out of deep feeling or the need to preserve a moment, a thought, a fantasy or a dream will be read at a later moment on a subsequent day and fall into a meaningful perspective. Some yield up their meaning only when we chance upon them much later.

This section is written with some hesitation. It contains tools and approaches for exploring the journal. It is not meant to be a mechanical press for you to use to squeeze every last drop of meaning out of your journal entries. Meaning comes like fruit, which when mature is easily plucked or drops from the tree. And so I want to liken what follows more to the tools with which one cultivates and attends to the orchard so that the harvest will be ripe and plentiful. Again, these are suggestions from others. Try them if you will, but let your own experience be your guide.

Beyond the act of writing, reading the journal entry is the next important step. Sometimes this occurs spontaneously during the writing itself or immediately afterward. The eye may jump back and forth during brief pauses of the pen, or, when a sense of completion sets in, return to the head of the entry and follow it once more to the finish. Often striking discoveries are made at once when the whole passage and the relationship of its parts are grasped in the panorama of this initial review.

There are other times when rereading is valuable. Rereading done within several days or during the week following the entry has a way of putting certain intense moments into a meaningful relationship with the course of my present life. Unattended needs become voiced and I am more likely to meet them. Dreams tie in with events. This rereading changes my everyday consciousness of myself with the result that I behave differently, not so much by a process of resolution and decision, though this is sometimes present, but simply because the changed perspective calls forth new responses.

Times for rereading will suggest themselves—follow your instincts. This may include choosing not to reread at certain times. For example:

> *I've been trying to avoid rereading my journal too much just lately because I'm trying to recover from the demise of an important relationship which is recorded in the journal and I don't think reading through all of it repeatedly is the most helpful way of doing that. But at some time in the future, I'll be able to read it without the pain that is present now and it will bring me insights from the time in which it was written.* (Portia)

Trust your instincts. Readiness and procrastination will come to terms with each other.

Besides the end-of-the-volume review described later on, I find that most of my rereading beyond this point is sporadic. Sometimes I go searching for something half-remembered which may be of use to the present. At other times I read randomly as one might flip through the pages of a magazine, pausing at items which catch the eye, whether a line or two or several consecutive pages.

Some people have a regimen of weekly or monthly reviews. This reading may be part of a regularly set aside time of reflection or it may stand on its own.

Voicing

Reading is enhanced by reading aloud. Hearing our own voice adds to a sense of ownership—we are in possession of our lives. *We* express *ourselves*. Some people intensify this effect by reading past entries into a recorder and playing the tape back to themselves. Replaying these tapes at later times can be a dramatic way of realizing for ourselves the great variety of feelings and shades of personality of which we are capable.

Listening for Voices

When rereading the journal it is possible that we will hear voices other than our own echoed in what we have written. Influential persons in our lives may have provided judgments, attitudes, opinions, threats, that are again and again reflected in our own thinking and consequently in our writing. The journal becomes then the place in which we can recognize when this has taken place. Things which we have swallowed whole can be examined and we grow in the freedom of choosing what we want to keep and rejecting what is not healthy for us.

Another question to ask when reviewing the journal is "For whom do I write?" Despite the essentially private nature of the journal there remain the internalized audiences, peers and parents, an adoring or condemning public in search of whose pleasure a great part of my life may be dedicated. This recognition too is a freeing one, not in that it delivers me entirely from needing or wanting to please certain persons, but it enables me to do it consciously and responsibly instead of being blown about by capricious inner gusts.

"For whom am I writing?" is a question I remember facing when I very first began keeping a journal. My first page reads in part:

> *This book is me. I am afraid I am going to try to make it beautiful, to write for the audience. Am I preparing to give readings, to publish? Perhaps. But I want to be careful not to write for an audience, neither the one out there, nor the one in me. It's going to be harder to deal with the one in me.*

Years later, I am still dealing with the audiences in me, the censors, critics whose opinions and judgments have become a part of the way I think and feel, but, by becoming aware of them I have lessened some of their ability to repress my ideas and energies and where I have not succeeded, I have at least brought some of the struggle out into the open where there is some hope of a negotiated truce, if not an ultimate victory.

While more will be said later on about the use of the journal in groups, one of the simplest, yet one of the most profoundly effective procedures for digesting and experiencing one's own journal entries is that of reading them aloud to a companion or assembled group. The presence of other people who support each other for this purpose, who are just there to receive without comment and enfold by human presence the voiced explorations of their companions, is a vital and creative force for those who share their work. This is the style of the Progoff workshops. In it even those who do not choose to share can find strength for their own writing from the assembled group and the voices of those who do speak.

While I do believe in and use an interactive model for group work, allowing and encouraging members to question and respond to each other, I believe the possibility of just reading to hear oneself and be heard by others without further comment or discussion should always remain a live option. I encourage group participants to use it when it feels right. Thus the decision to read or not read to others is followed by the decision to entertain feedback from others or simply to use their presence as a sounding board for one's own work.

Reading aloud, alone or in a group, can be a surprisingly powerful experience, triggering emotions of whose existence we were scarcely aware. Let them flow and lead where they will. The experiences one has during such reading are in turn affirmed by making note of them in the journal where they wait like clues for further sleuthing into the mystery of one's life.

BASIC STRATEGIES FOR WORKING IN THE JOURNAL

Certain devices can be employed over and over again to deepen the exploration of specific journal entries or to inquire into parts of our life and experience with the journal. This section will describe and explain their uses.

The Dialogue

The first and most popular of these strategies is the dialogue. It is the backbone of Ira Progoff's "intensive journal" approach and has a pedigree which reaches back to the philosophical dialogues of classical antiquity. It continues to develop as a tool of contemporary psychotherapy. To dialogue is to engage another in conversation, and this is precisely what we do when we dialogue in the journal. We set down a conversation just as if it were the text of a play for the theater. Two parties speak in turn responding to each other. For instance:

> *Mother:* *Don't you think you'd better wear your rub-*
> *bers? It's raining outside!*
> *Me:* *Gee, Mom you're always on my back. I'm old*
> *enough to take care of myself.*
> *Mother:* *I'm just telling you for your own good . . .*

As a journal strategy, the dialogue allows us to choose to whom or to what we are to speak. One may dialogue with virtually anything and everything. The list of suggestions given below is simply meant to sample the field in a suggestive fashion, not to exhaust it.

To create a dialogue one needs only to allow it to take place in the mind and set it on paper as it occurs. Sometimes the two parties will be already apparent, e.g., Me and My Husband or My Stomach and My Head or Me and The Car Accident. In this case, take a minute or two to identify in fantasy and feeling with each party before it starts to speak for the first time. The same approach works with persons or things which are already in the journal, e.g., with the Stranger in the record of last night's dream.

If the parties are not clear, focus the mind on whatever the issue or feeling seems to be and listen for whatever voices begin to speak to it. Usually these will sort themselves out and become a dialogue. Sometimes three or more voices may seem to emerge. If this is the case, after you have proceeded with them for a while check to see if several of the voices do not belong to the same party. If they do, combine them and continue. Here is an example of a dialogue:

Voice 1: I'm in charge of my life. I need to exercise the initiatives. Mine is the choice as to how I will select and direct my life.

Voice 2: You can't do that! You have commitments, promises, responsibilities to this community to consider. You're not free to act and decide as an individual. You have other things to think about.

Voice 1: But I say this so easily when I talk to others about their need to decide. Monday I was all full of good ideas for Ruth as she decided out loud in the car about her change of job. I find it so easy to tell others how easy it is to be independent.

Voice 2: There you go. You're trying to persuade others. If you were really convinced of your own freedom, creativity and independence you wouldn't need to reinforce by hearing yourself expound to others.

Voice 1: I'm letting us get off the track. I really need to hear each of us speak to the issue at hand. How do I approach the job decision-making for next year? I have so many "iffy" things hanging in the balance. I'm so comfortable this year at _____. Everyday I find more reasons and people to become attached to—to feel good. I hate being away from _____. I am afraid of a year alone at _____. I need the comfort and security of people I know around me to fill a gap I already feel is being created.

Voice 2: You need to get out of that thought and feeling pattern. You really have no choice to make. You know you can't take "no" for an answer. If you outline a scheme and it's not accepted, in the end, the final decision is theirs. They will even put the sanction on your "yes." It's very simple. Forget the efforts you need to make, the people you need to contact and convince and stay with the familiar that you know. You'll save yourself a lot of grief.

Voice 1: Funny, when I'm out here alone—no community person around—I find it so easy to be this me. It's easy to outline the things that need to be done, to exercise the initiatives. Then why am I so afraid to "get to" and do them? Why am I just "lazying" along waiting for something to happen? Why haven't I called F., written a job description, contacted B., etc.?

Voice 2: You know you're not going through with it. You know in the end, you'll be the good girl and do as you're told. You know I'm the stronger, deeper you. You know you're afraid not of all the things outside of you. You know you're afraid of me . . .
02/18/75 (Priscilla)

Allow the dialogue to come to a natural conclusion. It will usually do this if you simply let it flow out of your mind and copy it down as it goes. Trying to control, edit, or stage it complicates matters and hinders or prevents its conclusion. Let it happen rather than trying to force it.

Like most journal work, the dialogue benefits us in the doing and the reading. In addition to the normal reading there are two other approaches which I take when one or the other seems appropriate.

First, if my dialogue is written in such a way that one party titles itself as "I" and is addressed by the other as "you," a burst of meaning sometimes comes from reversing the pronouns when rereading, that is, saying "I" where "you" is written, and vice versa. The meaning will emerge in a particularly dramatic way because one identifies often for the first time with a long alienated side of oneself. This does not always happen, but it does occur frequently enough to be worth the effort.

Secondly, one may reread the dialogue to see if any of the voices it contains sound familiar. Listening this way, we may identify voices out of our past or present which we have interiorized or are in the process of making our own. Recognizing this benefis us by demonstrating sources of our thinking and judgements and giving us greater freedom in deciding how we place our own and others' priorities on our inner agenda. Often we parrot advice and old warnings which are no longer appropriate to our present situation and so hinder spontaneity and prevent fresh encounters with reality.

Some topics prove particularly provocative under this approach; here they are listed along with some of the more commonly used ones. You may dialogue with:

- People—in your past, present, future.
- Your job, hobbies, skills, career.
- Your body or any part of it.
- Dream and fantasy figures.
- Important moments and events, both personal and public.
- Literary, historical, artistic, religious works, figures and events. Places.
- Feelings, e.g., anger, joy, pain, boredom, fear, emptiness.
- Unfinished decisions, plans.

The Letter as a Strategy

Akin to the dialogue is the more extended statement found in the letter where the writer exposes his or her message and point of view in fullness and detail. For some people actual correspondence with a friend, advisor, or loved one serves as a functional equivalent of the journal. This demands an intensely close and trusting relationship. Often people who journalize in this way keep copies of the letters they send. It can also be a beautiful gesture for the receiver of such letters to save them, if the correspondent does not, and to make a gift of them at some later time.

The letters we are concerned with here, however, are not written for the mails. They are really one side of a dialogue, a strong and complete expression of one perspective or point of view. It is their intensity of feeling and uninterrupted flow of expression which makes them particularly valuable, exposing and acknowledging sides of oneself which have been long overlooked or put down.

The letter is just what its name implies, a message that begins with "Dear . . . ," and ends with the writer's taking responsibility for the piece by signing his or her name. Letters, like dialogues, can be addressed to any person, place, event, activity, or part of oneself or from any one of these back to oneself. With them we are able to marshall our feelings, ideas, demands and questions in depth.

Such letters in the journal, even when addressed to actual persons, are not written with the intention of being sent. They are rather devices to aid us in searching out and freeing our actual thoughts and feelings. It is not uncommon, however, for some or all of that which gets set down in the journal via letter or dialogue to find its way into our real conversation or correspondence. What was previously unthinkable or impossible, once written out becomes clearer and less threatening. If we have not dared to think or say something to another, it remains ominous and oppressive. We fear the reaction and rejection of the person to whom it is addressed or the consequences of our own intensity or passion in saying it. Affection and particularly anger seem difficult for many people. The journal letter acts as an intermediary recording the litany of things unsaid and absorbing the immediate overload of feeling without simply dissipating it. Once it is in black and white we may discover that it is nowhere near as fearsome as it was moments earlier as a catastrophic fantasy hiding in a dark corner of the mind. It now becomes possible for us to own the feelings and re-express them in an effective way to the person or other addressee of the letter.

Again and again I have seen the journal letter serve as an effective step on the way to an actual reconciliation of tensions and disagreements between individuals as well as for the resolution of inner divisions.

To write the letter, once having decided to whom it is to be addressed, it is helpful to focus strongly on that person or other recipient before beginning. This is most easily done by closing the eyes and allowing a vivid image of the other to come into focus. Begin to address that image, and as you do open your eyes and begin to write in your journal what you express. Close your eyes and return to the image if you get stuck. When it is available, a photo or memento can also serve as the object of concentrated attention to begin the letter or to return to at moments of impasse.

The variety of letters is infinite, limited only by your needs and imagination. Here are a few approaches you might like to try:

1. *The Letter of Introduction:* A way of preparing to present yourself to others. Tell what you like about yourself. Tell what you want of the new acquaintance(s), co-worker(s), situation. Tell what you are prepared to give.

2. *The "What I Never Told You" Letter:* Problems in relationships, family, work often arise when we consistently fail to say what we feel or mean what we say. The private letter written in your journal becomes a way of exploring for yourself the unsaid words of appreciation, fear, affection, anger, disappointment, etc. Often we swallow not only the words, but the feelings and ideas which have given rise to them, so much so that they do not remain easily accessible even to ourselves. We need the space and quiet of our journal to let them surface again. Becoming conscious of them anew we are able to do something about them in real life.

3. *The "Parting Shots" Letter:* A variation of the "What I Never Told You" letter, presented as a separate exercise in the second part of this book.

The Marriage Encounter Movement, a thriving interdenominational approach to enriching marriages and promoting the personal growth of spouses in marriage, encourages husbands and wives to write letters to each other and to sit down and share them. Journal letters which find their way into sharing can be effective means of community building on a variety of levels.

Associations

Free association is used in the journal as an approach to resolving impasses. Related to the problem solving device popularly known as "brainstorming," association makes use of the mind's ability to relate its contents to each other in a fanciful and unconscious fashion and to produce these as reactions to each other.

Brainstorming, which can also be used as a journal strategy for concrete problem solving, consists of focusing on a problem and trying to come up with as many solutions as possible, no matter how farfetched, extravagant or unreal they may seem. One expresses them or puts them down without making any judgement about their practicality, feasibility or the availability of the resources needed to bring them off. Only when the well has run dry and no more ideas gush up or when one feels that a more than adequate number of ideas have been expressed, does the sorting out and judging take place. While no single solution taken in itself may seem adequate or possible, the combination of parts and insights will usually yield if not an actual answer or plan, at least a clarification of the problem and what is needed to solve it.

Brainstorming, as I mentioned, is largely directed to external, practical problems, e.g., "How do I get to West 216th Street when the buses aren't running?" or "How can I keep the rabbits out of my vegetable garden?" Free association is a method of dancing around inner blocs and images until they are teased into resolving themselves or yielding up their meaning or until the dance itself sends us off in a new direction.

Suppose, for example, that I have an instantaneous and natural dislike for a person to whom I am introduced. This individual has done nothing to merit the antipathy which is rising in me. In spare moments I may jot free associations in my journal, that is, allow my mind without any conscious shaping or pressure to pour out and my pen to write down whatever images ideas or feelings come to me when I think of this person, no matter how random, disconnected or irrelevant they may at first seem to be. Often in this process one association will ring out clearly as an insight into the reaction I experienced, as in the example, my extraordinary dislike for my new acquaintance. Sometimes the combination of the associations will provide a key to understanding.

Association is a useful technique for almost any situation which is characterized by disproportionate emotion, where the feeling generated by a situation surprises me by being far more or far less than I would expect. This, it must be noted, is not a means for analyzing, explaining away or otherwise dispelling our emotional reactions. It is rather a clarifying strategy which helps those feelings to find their true target and to result in satisfying action.

Association is a particularly useful way to engage puzzling dream images or recurring fantasies. More will be said about this in the section on dreams.

Charting Periods, Rhythms, Developments

The technology of aviation has conquered distance with supersonic bridges. Electricity has made the night into day and brought not only the news of the world into our homes but endless entertainment as well. The price of these things is measured not only in dollars and cents but in jet lag, anxiety, insomnia. It is difficult to be in tune with a world in which the norms of nature and the inventiveness of humanity have such complicated relationships with each other. We consult clocks instead of our sense of what is appropriate to a given moment. We eat when we are not hungry and wonder why we snack at odd hours.

It is not our purpose here to mount an assault to overthrow time-keeping, though the desire to fight or drop out of the "rat race" seems to be becoming more common. We are interested for the moment only in taking our own rhythms seriously enough that we can live in a healthy and happy compromise with mechanized time. The journal can help us do this.

Each of us has rhythms of our own. Some of our contemporaries go so far as to assert that there are biorhythms which characterize our lives from the day of our birth and are responsible for up and down, effective and accident prone periods following each other in a recognizable and predictable sequence. It may be too soon to prove whether this is so or not, but with some care and observation it is possible for us to know something of the sequence of feelings and moods which we do experience. Whatever the value of biorhythmic measurement, astrological forecasts and other systems of prediction, here we are concerned only with what we ourselves can actually chart.

We might, to extend the metaphor, speak of this work as paying attention to the *climate* of our soul country. We, like the weather system of any given place, have cycles and seasons that follow each other with some regularity. They are never entirely predictable because new factors are always entering into our experience of ourselves, yet familiarity with the recurrence of certain rhythms rather than depressing us can be taken realistically as the basic and even reassuring given out of which we move.

It is possible to observe many variations of temperament and thus be ready to meet our needs more effectively when the moment calls for a change. We can for instance regularly look at our day and over a period of time gain some sense of when we tend to be alert and when we are tired, when placid and when emotional, when involved and when withdrawing. We can key into persons, events, activities and other factors which modify our feelings. Awareness of these things yields a twofold wisdom, a capacity to accept where we are at certain periods and go with their demands, and some power of change which comes from knowing the potential of certain things to affect our condition. In either situation we are "taking care of ourselves" in the best sense of that phrase.

Over the days and months it becomes possible to chart larger cycles. We can become aware of biological rhythms, the need for togetherness and apartness in relationships, times of aggressiveness or retreat, sexual energies, acquisitiveness and release.

Begin with what interests you or is problematic and keep a regular record of it and the circumstances which affect it. Do not do too many things at one time. Some of the basic strategies mentioned in this section may be of use to you here.

Besides plotting the ongoing rhythms of our lives as they occur, there are other useful strategies for capturing and seeing our developments from the past to the present, thus freeing our energies for future movement and new directions.

Ira Progoff has created two strategies which can be used for this purpose, the *period image* and *stepping stones*.

The Period Image: Sitting quietly one allows inner imagery and feelings to flow freely through the mind and body until at last one image or feeling settles in as appropriate for the movement of the present period of one's existence. It may be a knot in the stomach, a breaking out of one's shell, etc. This image is recorded and then expanded upon as one relates other persons, events, works, bodily occurrences and feelings to it to round out the period. This is done to situate oneself in the movement of one's life. The brief notes made around the period image provide material for more extensive attention later. This can be done with basic strategies such as dialogue and meditation (the particular form which Progoff calls "twilight imagery") and others.

Stepping Stones: These are the events which spontaneously come into consciousness when we look back on the course of our lives from the beginning to the period in which the present is contained. They are the framework upon which life has been raised in actual fact as we see it rather than by conscious design. The person setting down these stepping stones, sitting in silence, will record anywhere from eight to a dozen images which represent the periods of living that have brought us to now. This list is then reread and surveyed for any messages that it contains about the whole movement of one's life. Each of the periods there represented, beginning with that which seems most outstanding, can be descended into and probed in the same fashion as the period image.

A somewhat different approach which I have created to explore development is *graphing*. Using a horizontal time line and a vertical line which represents quality of experience (cf. illustration) I ask individuals to graph what they perceive now to have been the highs and lows of their life experience to the present. Any number of these graphs can be drawn, representing such things as education, career, the course of a relationship, level of self-satisfaction, feelings towards one's body, public and social engagement. The peaks and dips are marked with the events they signify and these highs and lows can then be explored by writing their story or by any of the other basic strategies. Such graphs can also be compared with each other. If, for example, one's satisfaction with work is far out of kilter with other dimensions of life or a relationship is seen to be particularly poisonous, this comparison frees us to focus on the real issue and by further journal exploration find new attitudes or come to healing decisions about it. A sample graph:

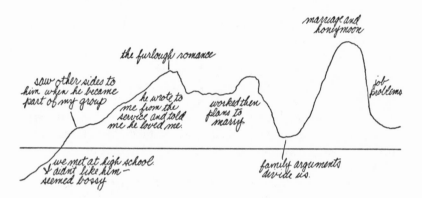

My relationship with Carl

marriage and
honeymoon

the furlough romance

saw other sides to
him when he became
part of my group

he wrote to
me from the
service and told
me he loved me.

worked then
plans to
marry

job
problems

we met at high school.
I didn't like him—
seemed bossy

family arguments
divide us.

Learning and Believing Squares

Learning and Believing Squares are devices for comparing what we have been taught about a specific subject, what we have learned through our own experience and explicitating what we wish to resolve about that same issue. This procedure consists in dividing a journal page into four sections by cutting it in half with one horizontal and one vertical line (or using four separate pages if the journal is rather small). In the first section use symbols preferably, though words or phrases will do, to indicate what one has been taught or brought up to believe about, for example, sex or foreigners or money or God. Use the second square in the same way, but this time let the symbols speak to what you personally have learned by your own experience, exploration or contact with the subject. Finally in the third square symbolize that which remains unknown, your wants, desires, the unresolved part of your knowledge, relationships, attitude toward the subject.

The fourth square remains empty. It is the place where you note the insights, perceptions and suggestions for action which result from looking at the first three, responding to them and comparing them.

More than just a values clarification exercise, Squares provide a glimpse of our maturation process as it has taken place with the matter we choose to treat while simultaneously furthering the process itself. The symbols and other contents of our three squares can be approached by other of our basic strategies for added penetration.

Healing Memories

Journal writing and strategies which take us into the past can, if we let them, become healing experiences. Allowing painful or problematic events to be staged again in the pages of our book may permit the long delayed catharsis to take place or lead us to the action which will lay to rest the bad karma of an unfinished situation.

Too often we see our past or use the past as a bundle of excuses to explain or justify who we are right now. It becomes the foundation of our resentments, tastes, enmities, the excuse for present behavior, good or bad. As long as we allow this, our lives are less free than they could be.

To heal memories with the aid of the journal, the trick is not to analyze the past but to help ourselves to reexperience it. Analysis usually means tracing our present back to some "because" in the past, e.g., "I am a poor speller because I had a spelling teacher in the third grade who didn't like me." The "because" may be true, but calling on it as an explanation or an excuse does little to move us forward. Often it is a justifying ritual for staying right where we are. Reexperiencing is another matter. When in memory and writing we face the situation once again, and fully feel its emotions, we can allow them and our response to them to fully run their course in the safe laboratory of our journal. There we can talk back to the situation and the people in it without hurting ourselves or others. This requires writing in depth and detail, feelingful as well as factual. Often dialogues and letters are preferred strategies for the final working out of these past scenes that come to us in the course of daily journal entries or are uncovered in graphing and stepping stones.

EXPLORING DREAMS AND FANTASIES

Dreams seem to have a variety of functions. Often they are *integrating* information from the past, the present and our feeling life. Therefore, they contain messages about our present situation and seek to affect our decision making. Dreams may also be *predictive*. Since they take information from our memory and experiences and represent it in new configurations to the mind, they are able to "add up" situations and actually or symbolically stage possible events or consequences to certain acts or activities. They may be more on target than our conscious efforts planning or foretelling the future. Dreams are *creative*. They not only lead us to a fuller apprehension of ourselves, toward health and mature identity, they also provide energy and symbolism for self-expression in writing, art and religion.

Fantasies share to some degree in these functions of dreaming. They are also more accessible to us for deliberate efforts at tapping other levels of our consciousness for alternatives, energies and personal resources.

What are the tools for a successful safari into dreamland? How can we learn about these strange flora and fauna and bring that knowledge back to our normal "civilization" of rationality and culture?

Here are six steps to the successful recording of dreams, originally suggested by British psychologist Ann Faraday and Princeton psychologist Herbert Reed, and summarized by Norman Brown:

1. You must *want* to remember your dreams. That presupposes that you value them, that they pique your curiosity—maybe even scare you—and that you wish to understand them. We almost all dream several times every night, so if you wake up in the morning without a dream, you've probably just not remembered one. Because dreams are strange, disjointed or nonsensical,

they quickly slip from memory. The sooner you catch them the better.

2. You can learn to wake up immediately after a dream in order to recall it and record it. Keep pen and paper (or tape recorder) and a flashlight by your bedside, suggests Dr. Faraday. Before you fall asleep, use autosuggestion: Tell yourself several times, "I'm going to wake up after a dream."

3. When you wake up stay relaxed, keep your eyes closed, and run through the dream until it is fixed in your mind. Then gently sit up, switch on the flashlight (or a dim light), and write the dream down in as much detail as possible. Add ideas about what you think the dream means, what previous events sparked it, how you felt about it and so on. These thoughts will help you decipher the dream's meaning later.

4. If you're a sound sleeper who can't rouse yourself by autosuggestion, use the alarm-clock method. Set a relatively quiet alarm for two hours after the time you usually fall asleep; each time you awake, set it for two hours later. You should catch at least two dreams this way. If you don't want to interrupt your sleep so often, set the alarm for fifteen minutes before the time you usually get up. Because dreams often occur then, you'll have a good chance of recalling at least one.

5. If all this nighttime activity is too much for you, you can recall dreams in the morning by waking up firmly but gently and remaining motionless, mulling your thoughts, moods, and feelings until you evoke a dream fragment. You can build on a piece of your dream until the forgotten elements emerge.

6. Date your dreams, and keep their descriptions, together with their interpretations, in a notebook or diary. Reviewing them later from the perspective of time will shed light on apparently ambiguous dreams and on dream patterns. Dream sequences can give you astonishing personal insights. As psychologist Carl Jung wrote forty years ago, "The dream is the small hidden door in the deepest and most intimate sanctum of the soul."[16]

Some dreams and fantasies are literal statements of wishes, desires, or dangers, or logical conclusions to courses of thought and action, illustrations of possible consequences. So to begin with, a dream ought to be taken as is and tested for its actual truth or literal predictive quality. If I have dreamed that my basement is flooding, I check the walls for seepage and the pipes for leaks—usually things that I may have peripherally noticed but whose meaning had not really registered with me. Unfettered with our busyness and customary ways of thinking, our dream awareness often puts two and two together to come up with surprisingly accurate reports of what's going on around us and its possible outcomes.

Sometimes such a message is present, but instead of being literal it is only thinly veiled in symbolism. Here a look at the symbols and what they suggest to us by way of association will often be all that's needed to crack the code. We begin by noting in the journal where the images come from. Usually our symbols are derived from recent experiences, things that we did, saw, felt and heard in the last day or so. The dream may be a likely commentary on our current events. If this fails to give satisfaction, move to free association and some of the other basic strategies of journal work related earlier in this chapter. Begin with what interests you most or causes you the most discomfort or what seems vaguest or hardest to remember. Talk to the different parts of the dream and have the various parts talk to each other or carry the dream on further by continuing its story in fantasy. These techniques may not exhaust the dream message, but they will usually suffice to extricate its basic mood and meaning.

While most fantasies are less "fantastic" than dreams, this is not always the case. But whether it is or not, the basic strategies are still good equipment for penetrating deeper into the meaning they bear. The meaning of others' fantasies and stories for us can be examined with the same tools. Pieces of literature, religious and philosophical texts can be related to our own experience and feelings on a level deeper than everyday reasoning by subjecting them to associations, dialogue and other written expansions in the journal.

PHOTOANALYSIS

Psychiatrist Robert Akeret has concentrated much of his healing practice on the information accessible to most persons in their family photo collections. That old album or shoebox crammed with photos can be a real key to memory and provide material for growthful reflection. Akeret's method can also be applied to photos and other pictures which we include in our journal because they have some hidden significance for us.

Here is the way Dr. Akeret suggests we question pictures for photoanalysis:

The following questions and instructions are suggestive; they are by no means complete. They are offered to stimulate your perceptions, to demonstrate the wide range of possible experiences while analyzing a photo, and to give you a basic idea of the step-by-step process of photoanalysis you can apply to any photograph.

What is your immediate impression? Who and what do you see?

What is happening in the photo?

Is the background against which the photo was taken of any significance, either real or symbolic?

What feelings does it evoke in you?

What do you notice about physical intimacy or distance?

Are people touching physically? How are they touching?

How do the people in the photo feel about their bodies? Are they using their bodies to show them off? To hide behind? To be seductive? Are they proud of their bodies? Ashamed?

What do you notice about the emotional state of each person? Is he: shy, compliant, aloof, proud, fearful, mad, suspicious, introspective, superior, confused, happy, anxious, angry, weak, pained, suffering, bright, curious, sexy, distant, blank, bored, rigid, arrogant, content, lonely, trusting, strong, crazy, involved, frustrated, attractive, docile, bemused, correct, friendly, hurt, spontaneous, satisfied, depressed?

Can you visualize how those emotions are expressed by facial dynamics and body movement?

If there is more than one person in the photo, what do you notice about the group mood—the gestalt of the group? Is there harmony or chaos? How do the people relate? Are they tense or relaxed? What are their messages toward each other? Who has the power? The grace? Do you see love present?

What do you notice about the various parts of each person? Look carefully at the general body posture, and then the hands, the legs, the arms, the face, the eyes, the mouth. What does each part tell you? Are the parts harmonious or are there inconsistencies?

Pay particular attention to the face, always the most expressive part of a person.

Learn to read any photo as you would read a book, from left to right, then downward. Go over it again and again each time trying to pick up something you have missed.

Ask yourself more general questions, as many as you can think of.

What is obvious and what is subtle?

Where is the sense of movement? (Or is there any?)

What memories and experiences does the photo stir in you?

How do you identify with the people in the photo? How are you alike? How different?

What moves you most about the photo? What do you find distasteful about it? Is there anything that disturbs you?

Try to define the social and economic class of the people photographed. What is their cultural background?

If it is a family, would you want to be a member of it?

Would you want your children to play with theirs?

If the photos are personal—of you, your family, friends, or associates—try to remember the exact circumstances of the photo session.

How have you changed since then? How have you
remained the same?

The list could be endless, but these questions give
you some idea of the approach photoanalysis must take.
As we begin to work with actual photographic examples,
you will see that it is not really difficult at all. It means
keeping your eyes open for new discoveries. It can add
adventure to your daily life as you become aware of the
implications in the media and in the books you read.[17]

INDEXING

Those who keep loose-leaf journals and rearrange their materials under various subject headings either in the Progoff method
or in some system of their own devising have a ready means for
finding what they want from the accumulation of notes making up
the journal. They will have more difficulty seeing their materials
in the chronological order and with the original connections with
which they were first developed. A number of people who have
worked with journal keeping over a long period of time have
confirmed my suspicion that for most people the divided loose-
leaf arrangement is short-lived and they sooner or later return to a
continuous chronological record.

The question is, then, can finding and relating items in this
continuous flow of personal material be simplified and facilitated?
One approach that seems to work is the use of different colors for
different kinds of entries. I have used and continue to employ a
red pen for recording my dreams. The problem with color coding
is that it makes consistent recording dependent on too many little
variables like the presence of colored pens that work!

A better solution to the problem is the practice variously
called coding, keying or indexing. A system of letters, marks or
symbols placed in the margin is used to differentiate journal contents. Each individual will develop her or his own variations according to what is of interest to the writer. Gordon Tappan, a
professor of psychology at Sonoma State College in California,
developed such a system which in abbreviated form we present
here because of its simplicity and usefulness.[18] These are the keys
he suggests and their meaning:

C = *Clues and hints:* These are entries which record flashes of interest or feeling which hint there is extra energy available in the experience that has been recorded, e.g., "I become terribly upset at Daryl's simple suggestion that I take the afternoon off" or "The sight of that small isolated cottage brought tears to my eyes as we drove along the strange highway." These clues lead to unknown parts of the self which are opening up to conscious awareness. They are marked so that a follow-up will be made.

IC = *Inner conversations:* These are entries which suggest that one talk with oneself. They are indications of where an inner dialogue might be carried on with different parts of the psyche. For more information about this, see the dialogue portion of the section on basic strategies.

S = *Struggles, worries, problems:* Pain and fear may really be the marks of growth points. These entries state daily struggles briefly and clearly without rationalizing them or explaining them away. This clarity may be the best way of highlighting their meaning for ourselves.

D = *Dreams:* Mark these for follow-up, using the instructions given in the section on dreams.

F = *Follow-ups:* Use this letter to indicate work that has been done in the journal in the search for the meaning of other entries.

TD = *To Do:* A follow-up action which carries the work done in the journal into action in the mainstream of life. These are not "shoulds" but vital impulses to expression, decision and action. Marking an entry with TD means we want to do something about it.

M = *Movement:* This letter marks passages which show changes, growth, new awareness and insights, learnings. These are the joyful entries in which we celebrate our aliveness and our healing.

To these, other journal keepers of my acquaintance have added such things as:

FAN: To indicate fantasies or daydreams.

H: To mark pieces of personal history, either straightforward narrative accounts from the daily log or memories and flashes of the past which seem to occur at provocative moments. (These may also be clues.)

MED: Meditations, ruminations, reflections, commentaries.

ST: Statements, a special kind of to do. Things I feel I would like to say to certain other people in my life, statements I would like them to hear but as of yet have not had the courage or opportunity to do so.

If indexing is a useful procedure for you, you might begin by trying this system and tailoring it to your needs.

REVIEWING THE VOLUME

At the end of each volume of my journal—the books I use have enough pages to last me about nine months before they are filled—I try to set aside a few days for intensive reflection on it. It's best when I can have three or four days to myself or a weekend away from my usual concerns and interruptions. Usually some opportunity provides itself even though I sometimes may wait a month or so after finishing the volume before being able to leave work and distractions behind to go back over it. When such a block of time failed to materialize, I have had to salvage an hour or two on a number of successive days to do my review. It is important for this review that the time in which it is done be not too scattered so that the memory is able to be aware of the entire period represented by this volume as a single movement in time rather than as disconnected bits of personal data.

The basis of this review is a continuous rereading from beginning to end of the contents of the entire volume. I try to read the book as if it were something totally new, bringing as little an agenda to it as possible. Usually this reading is alive with new insights, perspectives and discoveries. I use a few remaining pages of the volume or the first pages of a new one to jot down these insights as they occur.

Dreams read like personal fairy tales and, when seen from this distance, are often clear and beautiful stories whose meaning I intuitively grasp in new depth even though I may have wrestled with them before and coerced them to yield up part of their message.

As I read on I also discover parallel pieces, events which repeat themselves in new settings, in a change of clothes, with different people, feelings and moods which recur, reasons and "shoulds" which I tell myself over and over again, images and figures of speech which return. When I encounter these things, I make note of them too. As I read, the collection of these notes grows until at the end I have a rather substantial profile of habits, scripts and maxims which I have lived by during this period. I call this my personal mythology and find the process of extracting it to be the most productive part of long-range journal work. I know that I grow and change by rousing this personal mythology to consciousness in the journal review.

Somehow simply becoming aware of how I think and act is the strongest factor in my growing and changing as time goes on. It is not a matter of making resolutions about being or acting differently. Rather, out of the new perception, my organism takes over and moves in different directions just because it sees differently. Occasionally these perceptions mark significant conversions. More often they tend to be slight deflections or corrections of course and the journal later helps me to see that what seem to be the great changes are the combined result of numerous small deflections. For me, this is what real organic change and growth is all about—a far cry from the kind of moralistic injunctions and distasteful "training of the will" that I was brought up to believe as the only recipe for becoming a better person. Gritting one's teeth and daring new things may well be a way into new experiences and a way through emergencies, but as the constant condition of growth and change, they are not only unsatisfactory but in the long run destructive of both body and spirit.

The end-of-the-volume review is also a time for completing unfinished business. Actual forgotten obligations to others or unresolved conflicts which the journal has prompted me to remember come up for attention. Unfulfilled "to do"s are given renewed impetus. These are entries which when reread strike one as requiring action or further reflection. Sometimes they ask things that I was not ready to do or think, but in the time between my writing them down and the present I have become able to respond. Often writing them down was the principal step of bringing them into my awareness in a way that they began to quietly work beneath the level of my other concerns and come to maturity.

Part of the unfinished business consists of unresolved problems, dreams and fantasies that are still riddles, and "loaded passages," those that seem to have more meaning, energy or feeling than their literal content would promise. Associations, dialogues and other journal techniques can be used to explore these further.

There are other occasions for a major review of this kind besides running out of pages in the current journal book. Birthdays, anniversaries, new years, vacations and retreats are all possibilities.

In addition, times of major decisions and changes of direction suggest themselves as opportune for more extensive rereading. Marrying, moving, illness, grief and vocational choicemaking prompt second looks at ourselves.

A friend of mine who started to reread 18 years of journals on the eve of her marriage wrote:

> *Researching my journal past has been instrumental in opening my personality up to my self. Recurring themes that I've been aware of in a shadow mode have come to light. I see that certain characteristics have been constant since at least 1959 (my 12th year). For some reason, seeing the age & encrustedness of those characteristics has helped me to begin to let go of some of them, accept others & be happy about still others. Oh, sweet awareness!*
>
> *Looking back in to my old journals was more of an opening than I could have imagined & I stopped somewhere in 1964, unable to absorb anymore of myself for awhile.* (Sabina)

EDIT YOUR EDITING

Editing is the process whereby a book is prepared for publication. It involves making the text literally and grammatically correct or appropriate, trimming excess, irrelevant, material and rearranging what remains in a coherent and effective presentation.

Few people publish their journals, so this formal kind of editing is not our concern here. There is a tendency however to carry on this sort of fixing and trimming and reordering process and we should pay some attention to it.

Because editing, even this informal kind, is a finishing process, it may run counter to the purposes of the journal which is used for personal growth. All too often our conscious mind is editing and rearranging. Our journals often have as one of their chief virtues the fact that we include in them the things we usually leave out and so expand our consciousness beyond its normal limits and enrich our lives with new possibilities.

So the trick is more often to avoid editing rather than to attempt it. The habits of censoring what we say and do will almost inevitably attempt to insinuate themselves into our journal keeping as well. We will find ourselves holding back, choosing euphemisms and abstractions, unwilling to feel what we are feeling, let alone say it. We need to name things by their names if we are to meet them, struggle with them, be nourished by them, if they are to benefit us or we them.

The suggestion here is *edit your editing*. When in the process of writing in your journal you discover yourself censoring and hesitating, first of all try to be as aware as you can of the feeling which impels you to edit. Relax. Try to express the impulse or idea which you are tempted to edit in the original terms in which it suggested itself. If you feel blocked in this, it may help to write about the hesitation itself or the urge to censor. What fears, injunctions, persons is it connected to for you? What might you say to these? Here the use of the basic strategies of dialogs, letters, and associations might prove helpful.

Trust first impressions for their freshness and honesty. Jot down a first idea first even though a new, improved version follows immediately on the head of a new impulse and is recorded too.

It is clear that editing one's editing is not something usually done at a later date unless one is very much aware of an omission or an avoidance. Better to write about the same subject afresh than to contaminate or destroy a previous record with afterthoughts and changes. At times however, memories of events and feelings which did not get recorded when they actually happened either because they were not remembered or did not seem important will surface as significant when rereading the journal. If there is space, these might be added along with the date of entry, or recorded in the current sequence with reference to the date of the entry to which they relate.

If you find yourself very given to abstraction, there is a sort of editing-in which can be useful. It consists in moving from the abstract to the concrete when rereading a recently written text. Abstraction appears to be a contemporary malaise. It keeps us safe, uncommitted, uninvolved on one hand, powerless and vague on the other hand. If the target is blurry, kept out of focus, it's impossible to shoot—so too, if we use "head" words only, it is impossible to feel.

Reverse editing, then, is filling in the specific content of journal entries.

> *I found Bob interesting in a positive sort of way.* becomes *I put my arm around Bob today as we were going out of the elevator together. I half expected him to be embarassed and perhaps pull away. To my delighted surprise, he put his arm around me too and there was a distinct smile of pleasure on his face.*

Sometimes this sort of editing can be done immediately, the very moment we catch ourselves making a vague or abstract statement—following it with specifics. Or later, when upon rereading we find ourselves dissatisfied with the course of an entry.

PAY ATTENTION TO HANDWRITING

Unless we choose to tape or type, handwriting is the ordinary medium of recording thoughts, feelings and events in your journal. If, as we reread the entries, we pay attention to the writing itself, that is to the shape, size, smoothness, separation, style and relationships of the letters, words, and phrases we use, there are some simple messages which most of us can tune in to and understand. Even if we are not experts at grapho-analysis, it is possible to discern trends of energy and tiredness, of tension and relaxation, and to ask ourselves what it feels like to write in a certain way.

Handwriting, somewhat like tone of voice in speaking, contains subtleties of expression which we can learn to recognize and appreciate as they add gentle nuances to the contents of our journal. Changes in feeling and personality are reflected not only from entry to entry, but also over longer periods of one's life. I notice, for example that the small, tightly organized letters that I wrote with five years ago have given way to looser, larger, more comfortable ones. It is a change that, as I reflect on it, I see taking place in other facets of my life, and it pleases me.

I have noticed that when people speak from different parts of themselves their handwriting changes as well, sometimes dramatically. Experimenting with different styles of handwriting may in turn open the doors to different sets of feelings about ourselves.

CHAPTER 5 **SOME SPECIAL APPLICATIONS**

Learning, work, relationships, travel, communities—all of these are areas of life which journals may touch upon and at certain periods of one's life be particularly concerned with. The journal may be a tool to enhance one's classroom work or other learning situation or therapy. It may chart the course of a relationship and provide feedback for those involved. Written entries may serve as barometers of job satisfaction or as assessments of one's vocational preferences or goals. In this section we look more closely at some of these possibilities, offering some helpful techniques and approaches.

THE JOURNAL AND EDUCATION

Today, as I continue to keep a journal, I am above all aware of how my writing puts the dimension of personal experience into learning and growth in a way in which it was largely absent in the years in which I was being "educated." Educators, secular as well as religious, can abuse tradition by making it an object for consumption in its own right rather than using it as one of the keys to unlock the present. It is not insignificant that graduates are often given symbolic keys to which there is no door in reality. The door is experience, and without access to it the key burdens the neck like the proverbial albatross. Some of the qualities used to judge maturity in an organism are agility, expressiveness, productivity and fertility. These same qualities in students often threaten teachers who limit them to narrowly predetermined modes of expression. Meanwhile students, whose own experience is discounted, are expected to ingest others' ideas, values, procedures.. Psychic (and often physical) corpulence and indigestion often result.

To me the present controversies about the proportion of content and methods of teaching are secondary, perhaps irrelevant. The real issue is introjection, being required to swallow other people's beliefs, ideas, values and patterns of behavior without being given the room to test them against personal experience. It is possible to be more doctrinnaire with contemporary educational methods than Sister Eleanore ever was when she taught her fourth grade class the Baltimore Catechism to the tune of a hickory stick or Mr. Pettegrew was when he devoted ninety percent of his American history course to F.D.R. Education seems to be moving in a healthy direction, yet discrepancies between theory and practice are not hard to find.

Journals have become overwhelmingly popular as academic tools. One wonders whether it is just because it is the "in" thing to do or because there is a growing consciousness of the essential importance of the subjectivity of the observer to the total processes of seeing and learning. Journals are recommended ad nauseam in a wide variety of courses—to the point that one suspects that there will soon be a reaction against them, especially where they are used without the kind of care which preserves the privacy and integrity of the student who is asked to employ the journal as a learning tool. Where used well, it is well received. A professor who employed journals for many years reports:

> . . . Favorable feedback from students is not so surprising when it is realized that their journal represents a creative work which has put the student in touch with his creative powers. The journal becomes a vehicle for experiencing a basic change in self concept. No wonder a student feels that the most important thing he learned in college was how to keep a journal, if by means of the journal he discovers himself to be a creative person and his life becomes an ooportunity to give expression to his creative talents.[19]

A friend of mine who uses the journal as a teaching tool summarizes these ways in which the journal writing experience may prove personally rewarding to her students:

Self-directed learning: Through your active interaction with the course through your journal you will begin to see what is valid and personally meaningful to you. You will become more self-directing and responsible for your own learning rather than looking passively to an outside authority for all directions.

Self-awareness: You will hopefully increase your awareness of yourself as a unique person. You will discover personal assumptions and attitudes in which you are similar or dissimilar to your classmates and instructor.

You will increase your awareness of yourself as a communicator. By analyzing communication experiences, personal attitudes and skills, you will discover your strengths and weaknesses as a communicator. You can begin to turn even partial failures into learning experiences through critical analysis of them.

Active participation in class: The questions, insights and objections which arise from communicating intrapersonally in the journal can be shared in class. This sharing can be one of the most profitable parts of the course. You may even occasionally wish to share by reading to the class from your journal.

Experiencing the inner freedom to share yourself "YOU" with other persons and to accept their sharing of themselves will result in (1) increased awareness of individual differences, (2) increased empathy, (3) increased acceptance of others, (4) increased trust, (5) deeper levels of communication, and (6) additional resources.

Recapitulation and reinforcement: The journal will be your record of YOU and this course. You will be able to refer to it after the class has terminated for reinforcement of your learning.

Evaluation of personal growth: The journal will provide a record in your own handwriting of your personal changes and development over the quarter. It will provide a method for evaluating your personal growth.[20]

As in most places where the promise is great, the risks are high. When the journal is used and shared there is a very delicate relationship established between teacher and student, requiring patience, trust and honesty. One young woman recently out of high school in the course of a journal workshop was asked to write about what persons had enriched her life by caring, teaching, and delighting in her. She wrote about a teacher who through the use of the journal helped her to come to a new level of personal communication.

> *The first one was an English teacher my junior year. It was a mass media class. Although we did many things in class day to day, our weekly assignment was writing a journal. Our teacher was pretty cool. She was only 22 and I could write my true feeling to her and anything else I wanted. She would write back to me. It was like writing to myself but my journal could talk back. She was very open in what she wrote. And through our writing we got to know each other but face to face we barely looked at one another. But we could touch each other with our written words and that seemed to be enough.*
> (Annette)

Some suggestions about using the journal in group settings are given in the following section. These, particularly with the notes on privacy, will be of help to the educator who is considering the introduction of the journal into some dimension of coursework.

THE JOURNAL IN GROUPS
Personal journals can be used in a group context where interaction takes place around the material which individuals have written and chosen to share. Journals have been used in groups for educational, professional and therapeutic purposes. Many are written with the explicit intention of being shared or even published. While much can be learned about journal keeping from the experiences of those who have done it in this way, (person and vocation inevitably overlap in personal journals as well) for brevity the treatment here is limited to *personal* journals shared in a

group setting. Those who use or encourage journals for different purposes will find, however, that what is said here is applicable in some degree to the possible personal dimensions of other forms of journal keeping.

Here the focus is on interaction. Some group journal sharing, most notably the "intensive journal" approach of Ira Progoff, occurs at a quite different level. The group is present but does not interact; rather it serves as a nest of human support for the work that individuals do both privately and aloud in an assembly of people. This kind of group involvement is discussed in the section on voicing in Chapter 4. Finally, in our discussion "group" will mean anything from two people committed to a process of journal sharing with each other to a dozen or so people who meet for this purpose (the upper limits correspond with those governing the effectiveness of any interaction group—exchange is impeded by rising numbers).

The personal journal is not a thing which is written to be shared. Often the very motivation for writing is the practical or emotional impossibility of articulating or sharing certain things in any other way, things which are nonetheless crying for expression. Building up our private sphere has already been mentioned as one of the fruits of private journal keeping.

This raises what I consider to be the fundamental issue of using journals in settings beyond the individual's own private writing, the tension between confidentiality and sharing. What makes a diary or journal so powerfully human and compelling is its personal quality. Because it is personal and private, it is the place where the individual is free to express himself or herself with perfect freedom. Nothing need be too intimate or secret for the journal. This makes its contents at times extremely sensitive and confidential. The journal's sensitivity can be respected only if the individual is absolutely certain that he or she will never be commanded or coerced into divulging any of its contents. What is shared in educational, religious or therapeutic situations must be volunteered out of a sense of growing personal freedom and a personally generated desire for interaction. This is as true of adults as it is of children, although the latter are more vulnerable to manipulation. Adults will feel tricked, cheated and angry, and they have every right to, if they experience themselves caught in an emotional striptease. Children's minds are not protected by definitions of statutory rape, as their bodies are. Forced revelations leave them confused and ashamed. Their anger often comes only later in the form of a deep-seated resentment to the teachers, parents, school or church, the persons and institutions which hurt them under the guise of helping.

On the other hand, freely chosen sharing with the individuals of one's choice is capable of promoting personal growth, a capacity for feeling and intimacy, community and caring. Sharing is always a risk, but some risks are worth taking and will be taken more frequently if they result in healthy experiences.

Interaction is an essential condition of our personal being and maturation. It is the avenue in which we encounter and influence the identity of others. Often the potential of encounter fails to be realized because we become ritualistic and superficial in our exchanges with each other. What we really feel goes unsaid, which means that grievances go unredressed and needs unmet, rich insights and unique discoveries remain hidden. Spiritual direction, personal growth and community formation all require authentic personal input for success. This means the unfolding of the inner person in communication with others with all the concomitant risks that entails. The journal can be utilized in this process most effectively precisely because it is created innocent of this purpose. Its power is that it belongs to the individual, so that when one does freely choose to risk sharing, the source is authentic. This is the chief benefit of journal sharing. The individual benefits of private journal keeping remain but a new dimension is added.

To some it may seem as if I am speaking out of both sides of my mouth. How can a journal be free of contamination by the presence of peers and authorities when it is initiated in a group, workshop or classroom setting where sharing is encouraged? It is not easy, but, I insist, it is both possible and essential to achieve an atmosphere in which the participants know that the leadership is sincere in respecting privacy and convinced that preserving and promoting the sanctity of individual work is a fundamental priority, valid in itself, even in those cases where no interaction whatever takes place.

I have led groups and taught classes where certain individuals regularly chose to get up and leave to reflect on their own

work when the opportunity for sharing and discussion sharing
was announced. They got as much support from me as those who
remained.

In relationships, groups and counseling situations, journal
keeping can be an enormously powerful tool for the simple reason
that it exteriorizes parts of the individual's actual inner process
which are relevant to the interactive situation in question. Interactive groups or situations can give reinforcements which individuals cannot find as readily for themselves. In all such groups
absolute freedom not to share must be actual, so that the individual continues to write for himself or herself without censoring
or editing for an outside audience.

The leader of a group using journals has two issues to bear in
mind. First he or she must respect the individual's right to choose
to be or remain in a class or group and the person's willingness to
work at different levels with various members of the group. Particularly in educational settings where requirements may be more
rigorous, if a journal is to have *personal* dimensions in its writing,
there must be other alternatives to group sharing or the students
must be warned not to enter anything into the journal that they
would not be willing to share. They must also have the right to
delete or edit the record before turning it over to a professor or
discussing it with others.

Secondly, the teacher or counselor working with a journal
group responds to sharing not by assuming that he or she knows
better what the sharer needs, but by offering what he or she has
that seems appropriate, and allowing the other to freely take or
reject the offering. In this way the educator or facilitator will
model the approach which is desirable for a group of this sort.
Personal and religious growth is an unfolding which is stunted by
the imposition of others' answers. Others' answers may be tried,
experiemented with, and thus become useful in whole or part.
Effective educators and advisors know how to avoid falling in
love with their own ideas and procedures and how to return to the
students' agenda when occasionally they do have such a romance. Moreover it is very helpful if the leader does not exempt
himself or herself from the process, but also writes and shares
when it feels right.

Along with all the other written forms of exercises that

people come to share in groups, journal keeping encourages precision of expression and gives people a springboard for getting into discussion with each other. This is a secondary but not negligible benefit of the process. Having something concrete, prepared, in front of one's self is a particularly valuable ticket of entry into discussion for persons whose shyness or uncertainty gives them difficulty when they attempt to speak or express feelings extempore in groups. Everyone has experiences, so no one need feel left out. This is the same power found in the written values clarification methodologies which have been used so successfully in the field of education. Journal keeping, however, has a greater potential for taking issues as deeply as one wants to go with them. Often the journal process can be begun with individuals and groups with the help of the curiosity and engagement generated by values clarification strategies because these truly consult the individual on his or her experiences and feelings. What is important is that we not demand changes of each other but promote the awareness and the support that makes change possible when we are ready to risk it.

Risking is Risky

"Sharing" and "risk" are shopworn containers, too often repeated words whose meaning has dribbled out and become lost. Let's be clear. Exchanging intimacies is taking our lives in our hands and putting them in someone else's. It's handing another the keys to your new psychic car, climbing into the death seat and saying, "Let's go." Anything can happen from a fender bender to a total wipeout. You could get hurt. Or, the driver may take you to landscapes and wonders in your soul-country where you've never been before. Or, what is more likely, you may simply by sharing lighten the burden of the long transcontinental grind we each steer from birth to death. Each journey is unique, but traveling companions may significantly affect the route we choose. The analogy limps, but it does speak to the seriousness with which we must decide with whom we share the keys to our inner selves. Trust is built up slowly and based on experience. Not everyone who has a valid license gets our car, just the ones we know of, try and approve.

Journal sharing makes individuals vulnerable to each other.

This is a life and death matter. It can mean more life, it can result in hurt. Above all, individuals must be and know that they are in charge of their own process. Those who engage in journal sharing and those who promote it in groups as a personal growth tool must do everything in their power to prevent coercion and manipulation. This is especially true of those in a directive, counseling or teaching capacity, who have an aura of authority naturally accruing to their position. When, for example, I teach a course which recommends the keeping of a personal journal and the possibility of sharing from it, I make every effort—much more than an initial statement of intent—to continually see that people are in such a group only because they want to be, and, once within the group, that they continue to have the liberty to share or not share or even withdraw from participation, no questions asked, without any penalties, at any time.

It has often been observed that we sometimes share with strangers especially in telling about ourselves, what we fail to share with intimates. Working with a group of strangers (much personal growth work in the human potential movement is done this way) gives freedom and new starts on ourselves, but it is so much easier both to take responsibility or be irresponsible when the relationships will probably be transitory as opposed to those we are literally or figuratively wedded to. Retreats among strangers may give us a new start in life but the substance of that start is actualized where we make our home. Journal sharing is a lever which may make it possible to move stones we couldn't budge before; it is still time-consuming, backbreaking work to clear the field.

Teaching Journal Keeping

Diarists must often be taught how to write—not grammar, spelling and punctuation, but the signs, metaphors and images which best capture experience and make it capable of living again. This vividness is truth made accessible. Beyond this little is needed, yet an infinite number of styles and techniques are possible. My own approach to teaching journal keeping has included the use of a large number of facilitative devices, exercises which individuals and groups can use to stimulate the exploration of various areas of personal experience, faith, feeling, perception, valuing, environments, acts, events, etc. They are nudges, or "openers," ways of overcoming inertia and blocks to feeling, memory and expression. Many are capable of being reused and expanded and built upon by the persons using them. The second half of this book is a collection of such devices. Most can be used in group situations as well as by individuals writing alone.

USING STRATEGIES IN GROUPS

As you consider the exercises provided in detail in Part II, "Exploring Soul Country" and in the "Excursions in Brief" for use in a journal keeping group or educational situation, do not overlook the possibility of also employing the materials which are found in the first half of this book. There are, for example, helps for starting a journal in the chapter of that title and particularly useful and repeatable approaches in the section on basic strategies in Chapter 4. Dialogues, letters, associations, charting, along with learning and believing squares make excellent material for group sessions both as principal exercises and follow-ups to other experiences.

THE JOURNAL ON THE JOB

The line which divides a personal journal from a professional one may be thin indeed, so thin that at times it exists only in the mind and intention of the writer. In both personal and professional journals some seepage from either side is inevitable. Our work and play, the people we labor and live with cannot be tightly compartmentalized though at times we attempt it.

Keeping a record of job satisfaction, accomplishments, problems and noteworthy happenings can be not only a good way to monitor your feelings and choice about employment, it can also pay off in a variety of tangible benefits. Starting a journal or using an existing one to record what you learn and feel, particularly when an occupation is new, can be a real help in deciding whether you want to stay with it and in choosing which of its options and possible directions are ones you wish to follow.

Beginning such a record can be helpful for old jobs, too. It can revitalize work that seems to have gone stale as well as be the impetus toward vocational change if it appears that your inner inclinations have become so out of synchronization with what you are doing that some change of direction, employment or profession is in order. The record of what you like and dislike will also be a significant resource for knowing your mind if and when you decide to seek employment elsewhere or set out on an entirely new venture.

Drawing a graph (see graphing, p. 69) of your story of job satisfaction can be revealing and a source of motivation for continuance or change. If, for example, this line is far out of kilter with how you feel about yourself and your relationships with others, something should be done about it.

A record of one's successes and failures, triumphs and frustrations, problems and breakthroughs, can be used in very concrete ways to affect the job itself. Because of its specificity and objectivity, such a record passes out of the classifications of bragging and griping and becomes data that higher-ups will respect when decisions are being made to restructure jobs, improve efficiency and working conditions, and reshape the responsibilities of various employees. It will provide solid material for writing a job description for a successor and enrich the writing of your own resumé when you decide to relocate. It will provide factual arguments to support your request for a raise or promotion.

What we have said thus far is valid for just about any job. Certain occupations can profit even more from the journal keeping habit. We are not yet talking here about professional records, the kind that a profession itself requires its members to keep, but about the personal journal as it realistically takes into account the active working dimension of our days. Recording one's real feelings and reactions in most professions will provide incentive for the humanizing of those professions. Cold, hard, "objective" science and technology need on one hand the distancing which makes them accurate and effective but on the other hand require the regular reminder that they are the work of people for people. The personal account allows us to view how and why we do what we do, what we expect from it and how we see it affecting others. These are the human learnings that are absent from print-outs and statistical tables and without which the data itself can be threatening and destructive. The personal record of the journal can be our ethic at work, the place where experience and priorities come face to face.

Those whose work in the human professions requires them to speak publicly or in meetings, conferences, pulpits and classrooms will find in the journal an inexhaustible supply of experiences, anecdotes, examples, illustrations and conversation starters. Stories are political persuaders as well as lively entertainment.

Vocation, profession and work provide just one more area where the journal can feel its perceptions back into life in an active way as a source of enrichment and an agent of change.

THE COMMUNITY JOURNAL

Journals are written by participants as events happen; histories are produced with an after-the-fact quality with the altered perspective of time and a methodology explicit or implicit about what is important. Today we tend to write histories about communities even when the events we describe are still afoot. What journals and logs continue to be made usually look like skeleton records of events with emphasis on time and place, like the technical records of a ship's or plane's routine maneuvers. When human drama or feeling enters in, it is by exception or by accident. The existential quality is even then often lacking. Our newspapers and newsletters and magazines are called "journals." Yet while they record the day by day, the very volume of their contents, their efforts at an "objective" style and the variety of purposes and perspectives make it hard for us to see them as the bearers of "our" story.

It seems to me that there is still room for journals which chronicle the lives of communities, families and groups of people; that these could contribute significantly the precious gift of identity which melts away like sand under our feet as the waters of change break on our shoreline.

I have no experience and so no pros and cons to share on this subject other than to remark about the poignant literary contact such journals have given me with my ancestors and fellow humans from ages past. Even fictional chronicles tell more truth than no record at all—who could fail to be moved by the story of the community journal woven by Elie Wiesel in his novel, *The Oath*? I tell those who keep journals that it is very important to write and speak in the first person, to accept responsibility in this way for one's feelings and deeds. But these "I"'s must be at work establishing real "we"'s. The creation of "we" as well as "I" journals could be a most precious bequest to our children or those who follow us in vocation and faith. Nonphilosophical, personal statements free us from slavery to ideologies. In them we listen to people, not to principalities and powers. Why else should we find them so interesting?

Zalman Schachter told me the story of finding a small scroll in the corner of the ark of a synagogue where he was leading a Bar Mitzvah class. Next to the sacred volumes of the Torah was this minor piece which on inspection turned out to be a journal of the things that happened to another Bar Mitzvah class some twenty years before. The feelings of excitement, continuity, belonging which occurred across a generation as this scroll was unrolled and read was a youthful parallel to what must have been the experience of Nehemiah a millennium and a half ago when the Torah was found—Aha! This is who we are, these are the people we're related to, descended from. The community journal is a sacred book, so it is not astounding that a number of the world's sacred scriptures are or originated in whole or part as community records and stories. We should not be surprised to find such books in temples and churches as well as libraries and archives.

Are there so few community journals because there are so few true communities, or so few satisfying communities because people fail to record or even notice the events we experience together? If, as Hannah Arendt observes, our contemporary alienation is from both history and nature, we can take a step toward healing by the meditative recording of what we see taking place in each.

Some friends of mine have a bathroom family journal. There, where creativity is connected with primal urges, the propensity to scrawl graffitti on the walls is satisfied by the book which becomes a vehicle of family communication. Things unsaid get said, and since each member of the family visits the room regularly, they get said to each other. Occasionally the volume is detached from the cord which holds it conveniently and is brought out for a fuller sharing of the joys, pains, humor, pathos, stories and messages which make up family life.

Helen Rezatto reports on another interesting form of family journal in this way:

A family journal-scrapbook combination now circulating around the country to fourteen contributing families is an ingenious method of sharing news and memories devised by a remarkable clan of Browns. Mother Brown, who raised nine children to be inventive on an isolated farm in the Utah Rockies, used to say when her brood became too noisily creative, "Oh my, what a hub-bub!"

Now, The *Hub-Bub* is the title of a homemade memory book for which big and little Browns submit material all year, then wait impatiently to admire the final result of their combined efforts through a round-robin procedure.

Imaginatively edited by Mrs. Betty Brown Dorland of Tarrytown, New York, this yearly roundup of Brownerama presents family news in many forms—"letters to everybody," newspaper clippings, photos, original cartoons—and under many categories—graduations, weddings, births, vacations, "brag department."

Innumerable Browns vie for their contribution to be chosen by Mrs. Dorland as the prize-winning Anecdote of Olden Days, Best Description of a Vacation, or the Best Reminiscence like "What Was Kept in the Locked Drawer of Grandma's Box." Family documents are there—including both Grandpa's will and his fishing license.

Pure nostalgia, preserved under plastic protectors, are displayed in Brown's "believe it or not" section: a turkey feather, a pig's bristle, strands from the old hall rug, scraps from Mom's apron, bits of parlor wallpaper—even a sliver from the old outhouse.

Mrs. Dorland, who believes collecting and arranging this memorabilia is more fun than work, commented, "We think The *Hub-Bub* is an enjoyable way for our big friendly family to keep in touch with each other and with our Good Old Days." The round-robin regulations are that each family can keep the book two weeks before mailing it on to the next name on the list. A shirttail

Brown relative thought it worthwhile to drive over 100
miles for a look at the fabulous *Hub-Bub*.[21]

There is no finer way to show our appreciation for another
human being than recalling treasured memories, things that they
would have forgotten and perhaps we ourselves would have, too,
except that some jottings exist in our journals to remind us of
precious moments, the little things which once made life beautiful
and which now recalled become a real gift of gratitude. What we
once wrote of others in good times may bolster us in hard ones
and what we wrote on difficult days will enhance our enjoyment
of present progress.

To these special applications of the journal keeping process
you are invited to add your own. Freedom of imagination and a
little patience are all that is required to make it work for you.
Happy jotting!

PART II
EXPLORING SOUL COUNTRY

INTRODUCTION

Travel, Exploration, Discovery — nothing is more exciting to me than what these words stand for. Marco Polo, Columbus and Apollo Astronauts are latecomers to a tradition which began I suspect the moment some prehistoric ancestor found enough gestures and words to explain to her companions what she had seen when a strange place beckoned her beyond the limits of her serendipitous food gathering.

Journeys may someday be interstellar. They may also be infinitesimal, as when the trained eye of the biologist follows the movements of a microscopic specimen across its minute field. Some humans are poets and contemplatives who do not journey far in miles but discover hidden universes in the commonplace. Others are insatiable travelers who have lost the sense for newness and no number of journeys will reveal anything to them. Children explore each others' bodies and true and playful lovers explore both bodies and spirits. Outward journeys blend with inward journeys. Some clasic travellers such as Jason and Odysseus have left us in their adventures a whole mythology telling us about the journey through life. So also the star ship "Enterprise." Wander and wonder!

Discovery is the theme of this collection of journal exercises, "Exploring Soul Country." Our objectives will be to discover and explore, to chart the features and chronicle the story of our personal landscape, the world as we discover it both around and within ourselves.

The use of metaphors like "Soul Country" is more than a stylistic extra, a catchy phrase or an organizational device. In actual practice, the concept of ourselves and our world as a "Soul Country" allows a certain amount of fantasy and poetry to

emerge and encompass the events of our everydayness. Expressing ourselves with metaphors and analogies enables some of our
deeper feelings to emerge in symbols. The concreteness of symbols captures qualities of our experience in a vivid form where
they can be dealt with more productively than our colorless habits
of speech frequently permit. This is especially true if we are given
to making abstract statements about ourselves and gener-
alizations about our world. What follows in this second section of
our approach to journal keeping is a set of exercises which can be
used as vantage points on one's own experience in the course of
working with the journal. For those new to the journal they will
provide an introduction to personal writing by asking provocative
questions and lending some initial structure to the task. Most of
the exercises presented here, particularly the earlier ones, can be
used more than once. Sketching one's "Soul Country" for example is an effective way of getting a snapshot of one's present state
of self-awareness. I have found it useful as a monthly overview of
my personal world.

Because of the growing popularity of journal workshops,
notes have been added to almost every exercise under the rubric
"As a Group Experience." These instruct a group leader or
therapist in the manner of presenting each exercise and directing
a group in its use. These instructions diminish in detail in the later
exercises as familiarity with the process sets in. Used in this
fashion it is important to underline that the exercises *are not
parlor games*. They are capable of leading individuals to profound
insights, deep emotional release and sometimes dramatic
changes. This statetement is not meant to scare off potential
users, but to encourage them to stay in touch with enough common sense to know when they are in danger of getting in "over
their heads" and to seek reliable guidance when it seems necessary.

I personally have used these exercises alone, with individual
clients and with groups as large as a hundred people. I have
encouraged journal keeping partners and spouses to adopt them.
Each situation will, of course, require some adaptation. I hope
that the twofold presentation here for individuals and group leaders will provide clues enough for those who attempt them in other
circumstances to make appropriate changes.

While a competent and well-trained leader can enhance this approach, I have endeavored in this, as in much of my writing, to present workable techniques for personal growth that are not hamstrung by the limited availability and costliness of professional direction. Therapy and personal and spiritual direction are operating under an economy of scarcity. It is impossible for every person, even if we consider only those who want it, to have a private counselor, spiritual director or mental health professional. (This includes the professionals themselves.) We folk must learn to do these things for ourselves and for each other. Fostering trust and growth by loving, non-manipulative, reverential sharing of what we know and what we think we know is a task that belongs to everyone.

I urge professionals and non-professionals alike who intend to use these exercises with other individuals and groups either as a director or as a partner in the process to read carefully and digest what is said elsewhere in this book about group process and privacy. They are important for the progress and protection of those who use this method.

The exercises which follow are designed to last not more than two hours. An established group might want to add half an hour for random reading and sharing of other journal entries which are not related to these exercises. Individuals using the exercises alone may, of course, use them for as long and as often as they seem rewarding.

EXERCISES

1. SOUL COUNTRY

Take a full page of your journal and with colored pens or pencils draw a map of your soul country. Perhaps you conceive of yourself as a continent, a peninsula or an island, as a small or large nation surrounded by others. Shape your coastline or boundaries and then as you draw them, name the mountains and valleys, the lakes, rivers, jungles, deserts, cities, etc., the wonders natural and man-made. Try to be specific about yourself and your personal history when creating and naming these sites, e.g., "the volcano of anger at my father," "the island of loneliness at college," "the jungle of confusion about what to believe," "the joyful bridge which connects my soul country to my wife's."

Once you have completed your map, take a good look at it—this interior landscape seen in its fullness may be far different from the one you commonly present to yourself or others. You can use it as a matrix for a considerable amount of journal work. You may:

(a) Look it over and jot down the single word phrase or image which describes how you feel about the present state of your soul country.
(b) Take this word or image and expand it into a paragraph. Let your writing flow as far as it wants to.
(c) Write about what you particularly like, dislike or find missing in this personal landscape.
(d) Create a tourguide to the country you have drawn. This can be a lengthy project so do it for one feature at a time. The tourguide would contain such information as: place name; when it was discovered; its history; an accurate description of what it is like; current events and coming attractions; climate (i.e., the mood or feelings it evokes).
(e) Engage whichever of the features you desire with one of the basic strategies (cf. pp. 59ff.).

As a Group Experience

1. Allow about thirty minutes for the participants to draw the map of their Soul Country. Advise them in advance that there will be an opportunity to share from their work *if and to the degree* that each decides. With this in mind, particularly sensitive areas might be given names understood by the individual alone.

2. When the participants have finished drawing their maps, ask them to quietly survey what they have drawn. Then pause for a couple of minutes each time they answer one of the following questions in writing in their journals, as you present it to them:

   (a) What is my overall impression of my soul country? Is there a single word, phrase, image or symbol that would sum it up for me?

   (b) What one thing do I particularly like about what I see there?

   (c) What one thing about my soul country leaves me uncomfortable? Or, what would I like to change or see there that's not there now?

3. When this has been completed ask the members of the group to pick partners or form threesomes for discussion. Then prepare them for the discussion period with this information:

You will have about forty-five minutes to use for sharing with each other. Try to be sure that your partner or the members of your group get equal time so that no one is left out of the discussion.

The purpose of this discussion is to help each individual to see himself or herself better. You are not out to "fix" somebody else's landscape, just to aid them to tell it and hear it for themselves. So, provide ears, attention and even questions, but try not to argue for your own interpretation.

Begin by talking about what it was like to do this. Then, if you choose, share from your responses to the questions in number 2 above (mention them). Finally, if and to the extent that it pleases each individual, lead your partner(s) along the map on a guided tour of your country and tell him, her or them as much as you want to about how the various places got their names, what has and will go on there, the climate, etc.

There are several rules for this part of the sharing. Guests

*are very privileged in being allowed to tour this very unique coun-
try. There are three conditions of your visit that you must
scrupulously observe.*

*(a) Guests should not raise questions about things that they
themselves would be unwilling to speak about in their own country.*

*(b) Wherever internal security requires it, your host will tell
you that you are approaching a sensitive restricted area and you
cannot be permitted to proceed any further with questions.*

*(c) Take no photographs, souvenirs, or recordings. What
you have seen and heard is meant for you alone as a privileged
traveler and should be kept in strictest confidence.*

4. At the end of this discussion, assemble the entire group
together and, for the remainder of the time, allow individuals who
wish it to say in a few words what this experience was like for
them. Remind them to observe the "take no souvenirs" rule by
speaking only of their feelings and reactions and not about the
content of what others have shared.

2. TIME

Take a fresh page in your journal and draw the face of a
clock, without the hands, like the one below:

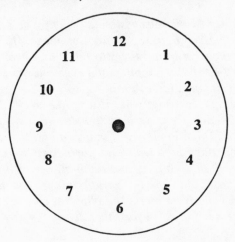

As you look at the clock you have drawn, ask yourself the question, "What time is it in my life?" Let the question sink in, repeating it if necessary, until you feel like the right time has suggested itself to you. Then draw the minute and hour hands on the clockface to represent this time.

Ruminate on how it is for you to be at this time in your life and allow these feelings and the facts that surround them to find their way into a descriptive paragraph. Here, for example is how one such paragraph began: "It is two o'clock in the afternoon for me. I am middle aged, like being in the middle of a busy but satisfying day at work. I love my job, but occasionally I glance at the clock and, like a shadow the thought crosses my mind, 'I am pretty much of a loner. Who will I go home to at quitting time, when the clock strikes five?' This anxious thought enters my mind more often than it used to . . ."

Write the paragraph that fits your sense of time and self. If the inclination to write carries you beyond a single paragraph, continue until you are satisfied.

Once you have finished your entry, the statements below will help you to explore your sense of time a bit further. Complete each one several times. If the completion wants to build itself into a new paragraph or statement, allow it to lead you as far as it goes. Here are the statements:

It is too late to . . .
It is too soon to . . .
It is the right time for . . .
I need time for . . .
I expect that _____ *will happen at* _____ *o'clock.*
An alarm is set for _____ *o'clock. It means . . .*

As a Group Experience

1. Introduce the exercise in the same fashion as it is presented for private journal work. Tell the participants, however, after they have drawn the clock, that they will have about fifteen minutes to write about "What time is it in my life?"

2. When all have completed step one, present them with the statements in italics above and ask them to complete each at least three times. Those who finish earlier than others might be encouraged to expand on some of their statements until the rest

are done. Tell the participants that they will have fifteen or so minutes to do this.

3. When the participants are done writing ask them to reread what they have written and to jot down the feelings and insights which come with this rereading.

4. As in the "Soul Country" exercise, ask the participants to form pairs or small groups for the discussion, remind them about the privacy and support needed for this kind of listening and that they should begin to speak about the experience and be free to share as little or as much of their work as each sees fit.

5. Reassemble the whole group for any concluding comments that individual members may want to make about their experience.

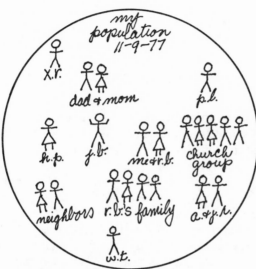

r.b. — you know I love you very much. I would like you to be closer to me. — as a matter of fact I'm thinking of asking you to marry me. I'm also worried about dad's and mom's opposition.

j.b. — get off my back. I've been working for you for two years now and it seems you don't trust me to do anything right. You're always looking over my shoulder and it makes me uncomfortable.

p.l. — I don't think I've ever told you how good a friend you've been to me. You've taught me much about myself, and especially been patient with my anger.

3. THE POPULATION OF SOUL COUNTRY

Who lives in your soul country? What are the passions and politics that make headlines and news releases in your journal? Let's look at the population. Abstract from the contours of your previous geography, and on a page of your journal simply draw a large circle or other shape which represents the people-space in your life. Use a small stick figure or face to represent yourself. Put it in the middle. Then add to the circle the other individuals and groups that are a part of your life in the proximity or relationship in which you sense them to be. Use closeness and distance, above and below to suggest this in whatever fashion it is meaningful to you. So as not to forget who they are, give them initials or names—B. L., Anne, the P. T. A., the parole board.

When you are satisfied with putting people into your space, spend some moments taking a good look at it. Then, in a word, phrase or image describe in your journal how the completed circle feels to you.

After this, write a brief note in your journal to as many of these individuals or groups as you wish, saying something specific in each case about how you feel about their presence, or what you yourself would like from the relationship, or what you would like them to understand or do in the relationship. Make these notes short at first. You can return to them later with longer letters or dialogues. Reread your notes and record any comments or decisions which follow in your journal.

As a Group Experience

1. Instruct the group members to draw the circle and fill it in. Allow about fifteen minutes.

2. When they have finished ask them to take a couple of moments to study it and note the word, phrase or image which fits how their piece strikes them.

3. Tell them that they will have fifteen or twenty minutes to

write short notes as described above to three or four of the groups or individuals in their circle.

4. Discuss, share and conclude in the usual way.

4. AMNESIA: WANDERING WITH AWARENESS

You are yourself in otherwise good health except that you are suddenly afflicted with amnesia. You have forgotten who you are, your name, your job, your roles, past experiences, exchanges with other people. The universe is a brand-new place. Look around you and begin to explore your world, allow your fascinations to run their course. Use all your senses. Describe what you sense as concretely as you can in your journal. No judgments, just description. Use whatever words suggest themselves. You have no censor looking over your shoulder since you have forgotten any such influences as a result of your amnesia. Take perhaps forty minutes or an hour to do this or continue as long as it feels right. If the season allows it, do it out of doors as well as inside.

When you have finished, leisurely reread what you have written, aloud if the circumstances permit. Try to allow each experience to become real for you again. Taste it as fully as you can before moving on. When you are finished, you might reflect on these questions, answering them for yourself in the journal.

(a) *What was the experience of amnesia like for you?*

(b) *Did restrictions from your memory or ordinary consciousness attempt to interfere with the simple flow of your awareness? What were these elements? What did they want you to do/not do?*

(c) *How did you feel after rereading your record?*

(d) *This sort of "amnesia" is available to you whenever you want it. Does the knowledge of this fact affect the way you see/feel about yourself?*

Remember that you can return to this state of amnesia at any time that it pleases you. Enjoy it!

As a Group Experience

1. Present the exercise in the same manner as it is introduced above, but tell the participants that you will call them back together in forty minutes. Tell them to wander and write alone in

their amnesia—there will be time for sharing whatever they want
to later on.

2. When you have recalled the participants ask them to take
a few moments to read what they have written to themselves and
to make note of any important observations or feelings which
occur.

3. Ask them to take partners or form small groups for discussion. Use the questions in italics on p. 111 to begin the discussion. If the participants so choose, they may read some or all of
their journal entries to each other.

4. Sum up in the entire group in the usual way.

5. *Variation:* At the outset, present amnesia to the participants in this way:

*You are now afflicted with amnesia. You have forgotten who
you are, your names, your roles, past experiences, exchanges with
other people. Your world is a brand new place. Select a partner
and take turns giving each other a descriptive tour of your respective amnesiac worlds. You will have to begin, of course, by giving
names to each other based on what you see. Look around you and
begin to explore your world, allowing your fascinations to run
their course. Use all your senses. Do not be in a hurry. Savor
each thing before you move on to the next. Do not omit telling
each other what you discover in each other in this state of amnesia.*

When this is over (about forty minutes) ask the participants
to take half an hour or so to write the answers to the italicized
questions on p. 111 and note any other particulars about the experience. Discussion of the experience and of volunteered journal
entries can then take place in the large group.

This form of amnesia can be used very effectively as a
shared exercise between partners in marriage, friendship or working relationships to find new ground with each other, new stand-
points for resolving conflicts and misunderstandings. In such
cases, encourage them to explore their perceptions of the other
person afresh, uncontaminated by previous judgements and experiences. These questions will help: What new feelings do you
have? What do you want to do as a result?

5. *VARIATIONS ON HISTORY*

This is an exercise to help you get in touch with the lost personal history of your Soul Country, with the events that formed you as they are seen by the people who were involved in them.

The procedure is simple. Set up "interviews" with the members of your family, your parents, elder brothers or sisters, baby sitters, etc.; anyone who had an intimate contact or connection with your past life is a possible source of useful material. Some people will enjoy the novelty of such an interview, but if you feel that certain individuals would be uneasy with this playful approach, it is still possible to approach them with questions like, "What was it like when I . . .?" As you interview them, take notes in your journal about what is said, asking for clarification about things you don't understand. Encourage your respondent to be as concrete and specific as possible. Another way to do the interview is to give these persons a cassette recorder for a time and ask them to reminisce on your past. Each person preserves a particular view of the past, so you will learn more by asking people to do these things separately and privately. Ask, for instance, your mother and father each to give you an individual reminiscence of whatever part of your childhood you would like to look at. In this way they will not be influenced by your presence or by each others' conflicting recollections. Instead of Mom and Dad arguing, "He did it this way," "No he did it that way," you will have the two records of the same event as seen through the eyes of two different people. If you do it with a tape recorder you may record as much of this as you want in your journal and seek only clarifications and explanations you desire from these persons after you have listened to the tapes.

This exercise may also be an occasion for dealing with the unfinished business we have with some of the people we "interview." Remember, you are getting *their* picture of you, often colored by perceptions and feelings that you cannot be responsible for even though you may have occasioned them. On one hand they will aid your memory of things you have forgotten, on the other hand they may bring along baggage of their own which you may have the opportunity to unpack together. Some of the basic journal strategies may be employed in doing this as well as in exploring the stories they provide for you and the memories and fantasies that these trigger in your imagination.

There is a variation to this exercise—it is one that you can do yourself separately or in addition to the interviewing. Dig out your childhood souvenirs, toys and photos, diaries, books, jewelry, etc. Take each separately, sense it and savor it and, as you re-encounter it, allow feelings, images, and memories to surface. What are they? How do you feel them connected with the present? Are they feelings and memories which you resist? Welcome? Where do you encounter shame and embarrassment, pleasure and joy? Note carefully in your journal what takes place as you come in to contact with each of these things.

As a Group Experience

"Variations on My History" is basically an individual exercise which cannot be easily confined to a specific time period. The accessibility of persons whom one can "interview" varies widely. Writing recorded and generated during this process, however, can be aired in time set aside for unstructured journal sharing.

6. GROWING UP IN SOUL COUNTRY

Once upon a time it was popular for parents and the teachers of children in their early years to encourage children to strive for greatness and to encourage their fantasies about being a great doctor, lawyer, writer, artist or scientist. Essays were assigned on topics like, "What I will be when I grow up," and "If I were President of the United States . . ." At a certain point, however, this kind of fantasy is no longer encouraged and a hard-headed practicality tells us that most of us are just average and encourages us to go about getting the tools which allow us to get our share of the "American way of life" and the attitudes which will keep us from "rocking the boat." Those who continue to harbor such fantasies through their teen-age and college years and into their careers (at a certain point they are prone to be labeled "delusions of grandeur") must do it in secret—their march toward greatness (and they often do go in that direction) must be guarded like a conspiracy and hedged in with protestations of humility, for society sees and punishes such ambition. But the truth of the matter is that greatness and excellence are possible for each of us. Sometimes they do not come in the form of our original childhood objectives, but more often they are modified by new wants and ideas. But they are possible nonetheless, and, what is more shocking to say, they are necessary, for as Abraham Maslow has put it so well, "If you deliberately plan to be less than you are capable of being, then I warn you that you'll be deeply unhappy for the rest of your life. You will be evading your own capacities, your own possibilities."[22]

In this exercise, we are going to return to fantasizing. Write a page-long essay in your journal entitled, "Who or What I am going to be when I grow up." It makes no difference whether you are eighteen or sixty-eight, just begin where you are at right now and allow yourself the fantasy that you enjoy most. Don't judge its practicality or feasibility, just allow your imagination to flow with it. When you have finished, read over your page to get the flavor of the whole fantasy. Then, reread it once more, this time noting: *What parts of the fantasy are realizable for you right now? What parts of the fantasy could be achieved? With what efforts? How long would it take? Do other similar choices seem possible and desirable?*

Make a contract with yourself to achieve at least some satisfying part of this fantasy by a reasonable date.

As a Group Experience
1. Present the exercise as above, allowing about twenty minutes for the essay on "Who or What I am going to be when I grow up."

2. Ask the participants to reread the essay and answer the italicized questions in their journals. Take fifteen or twenty minutes for this.

3. Discuss the results in small groups. Twosomes or foursomes are best. By questions and observations group members can help each other better articulate their fantasies. Toward the

end of the small group discussion, ask the participants if they wish to exchange contracts with a partner by copying them in each other's journals. If so they may also want to commit themselves to check with each other from time to time about progress toward their respective goals.

    4. Conclude in the whole group as before.

7. DEATH AND REBIRTH: SEASONS OF THE SOUL

    At the core of Christianity is the myth of death and resurrection, of dying to the old and rising to the new. This theme can be found in a variety of other religions as well. Some have similar stories of gods who die and rise. Often these are tied into the phenomena of nature such as the setting and rising of the sun, the passage of the seasons or the flooding of the rivers. These are powerful myths because they have a counterpart in our own experience of ourselves. They become valid for us when we reflect on how the cycles of death and rebirth exist, turn over and over in our days and years. Bill Bridges has noted that there is a difficulty with times of process and points of passage that

> . . . makes it almost impossible for us to deal with those two ultimate transitions, birth and death. We not only make them into things, but the first and last things—like the edges of the flat world that Columbus was supposed to sail off. If we weren't so linear in our imagination, we would see birth and death, not as the outer edges of something flat, but as the two sides of a single thing, a crossover-point at which the circle ends only to begin again. Like some old fuddy-duddy who loves to tell the story but always gets it confused, we are constantly getting birth and death backwards. It's always the dying that comes first, then the being born. We know that from the outer seasons, and we can discover it in the inner seasons too.[23]

    Let us use this myth of death and rebirth now as the jumping-off point for another journey into soul country.

Begin by making a list. Aim for about five items—if more readily suggest themselves, by all means jot them down, but try to get at least five. List the things that you feel are dying in your life, the things you feel diminishing, becoming less important, receding, separating, the things you are losing interest in, letting go of, things that seem just about over. Perhaps you once enjoyed gardening but are beginning to find it drudgery. Perhaps a friendship, a job, a marriage appears to be coming to an end. Perhaps an old attitude or feeling is changing, a belief or political alliance. Concentrate on things that seem passing but are not completely past.

When you have finished this, begin a second list of five or so items, this time of the things that are coming into being, things that are not fully a part of your life but which are rising, emerging, returning, becoming more important, more desirable, more frequent. A newly made friend, an interest in oriental cooking, a waxing desire to travel, could be examples of new life and direction.

Try to be as concrete as possible as you create these two lists. When you have completed them to your satisfaction, read them over slowly and carefully and pick from each list the one item which seems most significant or interesting to you. Let each of these two items become the subject of a paragraph or page of your journal. Tell the story of that which is waxing or waning, your feelings about it, anxieties, anticipations, expectations. Try to let your perceptions and feelings flow freely til they come to a natural conclusion. What is helping or hindering the passing of the old and the birthing of the new? What does this suggest to you?

If you have the time to devote to it you may want to follow this process for other items on your list. Is there a connection between the passing of some items and the emergence of others? Write about this relationship.

As a Group Experience

1. Introduce the exercise and instruct the participants to make the two lists of things which are passing and emerging. Allow about fifteen minutes for this.

2. Tell the participants to take a couple of minutes to look over their completed lists and to select one item from each which they find most significant or interesting. Allow them about half an

hour to expand each of these items into a paragraph or page of reflection.

3. Ask the participants to read what they have written and to make any further notes or comments which suggest themselves.

4. Divide into small groups for sharing and discussion, or, if you choose, remain in the large group. If you have worked in smaller groups, be sure to reassemble for any concluding discussion or comments that participants would like to make.

8. COMPENSATIONS

Human culture, from the simplest stone axe to the most sophisticated computer, consists of outward projections and extensions of human beings. Depending on their use, these extensions can be creative or destructive, tools or weapons. Humans are constantly extending themselves in new directions; they are also compensating for their peculiarities—this is another kind of projection or extension. For example, some tall people, self-conscious of their size, squinch down in their chairs, etc., to make themselves blend into "normal" surroundings; some small people make themselves noisy and aggressive to be "noticed." In each of these cases we see individuals compensating for what they perceive to be inadequacies. We make compensations because they are or seem to be of advantage to us. Some truly are; the enhanced tactile perception of some blind persons, for example. Sometimes the compensations can be detrimental. The tall person who squinches would be better served by learning to accept his or her size as a reality and a personal resource. We should be suspicious of compensations which stem from a negative self-image. We compensate for what we perceive as our inadequacies. Altering our perception can be as important as finding compensations and, more effective. Rollo May has observed that violence to ourselves as well as to others, emerges from a sense of impotence, from the real, or at least perceived radical inadequacy to fulfill a need. If we are to avoid violence to ourselves and others and to mature as humans, it is important to deal effectively with inadequacies and compensations.

This exercise will help you understand some compensation

functions in yourself. Begin with a few moments' reflection on the inadequacies or handicaps which you ordinarily see yourself as having. Jot them down in your journal. These categories may stimulate your reflection:

1. *Age: I am too young/old to . . .*
2. *Sex: I am a man/woman, but only women/men can/are allowed to . . .*
3. *Social background: If I were white/black/rich/etc., I would . . .*
4. *Possessions: If I had _____, I could . . .*
5. *Personal physical appearance/constitution: I am too short/ tall/weak/etc., to . . .*
6. *Mental, emotional, motor skills: I am too dumb/afraid/ awkward/etc., to . . .*

Next to the items on your list, or across from them on the next page, list the compensations which you have developed to alleviate the inadequacies. Be as specific as you can. For example:

I am overweight—I wear baggy clothes. I tell other people that John (who is physically attractive) is a dumb jock.

I cry too easily—I rely on anger to avoid tears.

I look too young to get a date—I wear my older sister's clothes and make-up.

Remember, when doing this exercise, you are not judging yourself. Judgment would simply make it harder to accept your capabilities and resources. Here you are looking at how the compensation function works in your life. It is a way of knowing yourself better and improving your resources. Some compensations may be performing splendid service. If you discover others which are inadequate, counterproductive or harmful to yourself or others, you will have a handle on them which will enable you to work differently. Doing this exercise will also give you the opportunity to review what you consider your inadequacies to be, perhaps to reconsider them as assets, or, at least see that they are inevitably a part of the resource for constituting the present and future you.

As a Group Experience

1. Present the exercise as it is above. When you come to the six categories listed in italics above, ask the participants to do at least two completions for each. Allow them twenty minutes or

so to work on this in their journals.

2. When this list is completed, ask the participants to proceed to list in the journal one or two compensations which they feel are functioning for them in each of the six categories. This will take about fifteen minutes.

3. Process this in the usual fashion in small groups and conclude with sharing in the total group. Ask the partners in the small groups to respond with honest perceptions of each other where this seems called for, to give these simply and straightforwardly, not trying to argue the individual out of his or her self image but simply as providing additional data for that person to work with. Others may perceive us as we see ourselves or, as is more often the case, differently. They may also see different compensations at work and thus challenge our assumptions about ourselves. Here we are trying to give each other as much useful information as possible.

9. WE—THEY

Relax, close your eyes and place yourself back in the first fifteen years of your life as you remember them now. Imagine events from those early years. Let them be staged on the screen of your imagination. At that time people were doing and saying things in your family, among your friends, and at school which provided the context in which your image of yourself was formed. Frequently this occurred by your being placed or placing yourself in "we-they" categories. Sometimes it was as simple as saying "us." At other times the distinctions may have been more subtle. Try to contact those distinctions now as they came into being in those early years, and as each comes to mind, jot them down in your journal.

Here is a sample of how you might proceed:

We—Us	They—Them
Black kids	White kids
My family	Everybody else who was wrong
The free world	The Communists

Continue until the well runs dry and no more we-they distinctions present themselves. Then, in your journal, describe some of the feelings and events that went along with these distinctions. Try to be as concrete and specific as you can. What parts still feel like you today? What "we" and "they" distinctions no longer fit? What new ones have come into being? Deal with these in the same way, list them and then expand on them. Write the stories which tell how these distinctions function in your life. Finally, take a look at the profile of you that emerges on the "we" side. Make whatever notes you want to about this.

As a Group Experience

1. Ask the group members to make their "we-they" lists. (Choose beforehand whether you wish to work on childhood memories or current distinctions.) Allow 8 or 10 minutes for this.

2. Ask each person to select the one dichotomy which seems most important or feeling laden and to expand on it in writing in the journal.

3. Discuss, share and conclude in the usual way.

4. *Variation:* When working in a group, you may decide to discuss your "we-they's" at length instead of writing them down. Do this in clusters of three or four persons. Tell stories if you wish, but be careful not to become just entertainers. Keep the story vivid and detailed. Try not to wander too far. During the story be sure to tell about feelings as well as events. At the conclusion the storyteller might say how he or she feels, having shared the story. Listeners might comment on what they felt to be the high points of the story both for the storyteller and for themselves.

10. COUNTERVALUING

Certainly we love and admire good men, saints, honest, virtuous, clean men. But could anybody who has looked into the depths of human nature fail to be aware of our mixed and often hostile feelings toward saintly men? Or toward very beautiful women or men?

Or toward great creators? Or toward intellectual geniuses?? . . . the greatest people, simply by their presence and by being what they are, make us feel aware of our lesser worth, whether or not they intend to . . . we are apt to respond with projection, i.e., we react as if he/such a person/were *trying* to make us feel inferior . . . Hostility is then an understandable consequence. It looks to me so far as if conscious awareness tends to fend off this hostility . . . I am willing also to extrapolate to the guess that if you can learn to love more purely the highest values in others, this might make you love these qualities in yourself in a less frightened way.[24]

We need to contact the power that lies in this mechanism so well described by Abraham Maslow. To do so, we are going to allow ourselves a bit of envy. Pick a person whom you know who is in some way successful, a person perhaps toward whom you already have some hostile feelings. Allow your feelings to flow freely about this person and his or her qualities which distress you or make you feel inferior. Write them down in your journal, trying not to censor your feelings or the language in which you express them. Feel free to express yourself as forcefully as you want.

Read what you have written. In your journal address yourself to these questions: What is the overall impact of it? What feelings does it generate in you? Reread it, this time noting for yourself the positive qualities and strengths, the achievements, attitudes or advantages of the other which may be related to your hostility. *What things in you are like/unlike the provocative qualities you perceive in the other person? If you allow yourself to see these things as strengths or at least as potentialities in the other person, how does this affect your perception, feelings, and judgments about him or her?*

As a Group Experience
1. Have the participants write the essay as described above, fifteen to twenty minutes).
2. Tell them to read what they have written and respond to the italicized questions.
3. Share in small groups and conclude in the large group.

4. *Variation:* If you feel that the level of sharing and trust is high enough in your group, instruct the group in this fashion: Choose a person in the group toward whom you have some hostile or jealous feelings. You do not need an all-out hostility to do this, just concentrate on some facet or quality that "rubs you the wrong way," that generates some discomfort. Write your page about this person and yourself and share as much of it as you wish in the large group. Again use the questions above to further your discussion. Remember, as you discuss these qualities in each other that each person has the right to his or her own character and to choose the directions of growth and change. No one needs to defend the way he or she is.

At times this can be done reciprocally. It is a good exercise for friends or spouses, a way of turning rough edges into assets for your relationship.

11. PARTING SHOTS

"Parting Shots" is an intense application of the letter writing technique described in the section on basic strategies. Here the image is that of the Lone Ranger firing over his shoulder as he rides away, chased to the edge of town by the dishonest saloon keeper and his gang. It is an experience of saying in the strongest most expressive language what you feel about a certain activity, place, relationship, as if it were your last chance.

Remember, letters of this sort are not written to be sent. They are rehearsals in which our awkwardness, new insights, and strong feelings, which would ordinarily be inhibited by stagefright, can come to the light of day for our own awareness and scrutiny. Fears about the power of our feelings and our catastrophic expectations of rejection can be brought out to the light of day where we can judge their true size. Because fears are often bigger than life, it is not uncommon for the person who has articulated them fully in a journal letter to be able then to bring that content to bear in an actual conversation or letter to the party to whom the journal letter was addressed. Even when our fears are real and well-founded, a letter of this kind may surface the energy and wisdom that is latent in us. We discover that we do have strength to wrestle with the opposition. At times also such letters reveal to us that what we perceived to be the enemy or object of our shots was only a front and our true target is revealed.

On one hand this approach may help us to finally make overdue decisions affecting our work or personal life. On the other hand, expression, even of aggression, can be healing. The journal provides a safe place for it to happen. What began as parting shots may at some later point explode us into a new and more satisfying relationship with what we originally saw as our target.

Here's how to begin. Imagine that this is the day that you:
• leave your husband/wife
• break up with a friend
• resign/want to get fired
• quit school
• stop going to church
• put down the book you've been plugging along at reading.

Choose one of these or address whatever person(s) or situation is most relevant to you. Take this opportunity to write a letter which fires some parting shots at whatever or whomever you are quitting or leaving. Say what you really feel without mincing words or inhibiting feelings, even if it seems like you're overstating your case.

When you have completed your letter read it to your self. Declaim it aloud if the situation permits. Use your journal to record observations, insights, decisions, plans which result from listening to your parting shots.

As a Group Experience
1. Present the exercise and ask the participants to write one letter, taking fifteen or twenty minutes to do so.

2. The exercise could be continued in the usual way in pairs or small groups concluding in the large group.

3. *Variation:* Remain in the large group and allow those who wish to read or declaim whatever they choose of their writing. Invite them to experiment with whatever degree of feeling seems adequate. Those who read may want to receive feedback from the other participants on how the parting shots strike the target.

12. DO YOU HAVE ANYTHING TO DECLARE?

This is a group experience. Information on using the journal as a notebook or scrapbook has already been given on pages 41-42. Present the exercise in these terms at the conclusion of the meeting of the group a week or two before you intend to use the exercise for discussion:

Earlier in this century a British literary critic, Maurice Baring, wrote a book called Have You Anything to Declare. *In it Baring pictured himself at death crossing the River Styx. There the customs agent for the underworld asked him, "Have you anything to declare?" The rest of the book was Baring's response —a splendid collection of all the precious and personally meaningful poems and scraps of literature that he had carried throughout life to sustain his spirit.*

Your journal can be a collecting place for the sayings of others which are precious to you. Perhaps you have already started such a collection. If not, the exercise which we will present now in preparation for our next session will give you a good start. Between now and when we next meet, assemble in your journal some of these items which are important to you: pictures, sayings, lines of poetry, songs or lyrics, letters from parents, friends, etc. Bring them with you to the next meeting of your group and we will take time to share them.

When the group gathers for its next meeting, introduce the discussion as follows:

At this stage of your journey through life, you are entering into the lives of other people, the members of your group. You begin to cross each others' boundaries. Imagine that you have arrived at the customs house. I am now going to ask you what you have to declare, to open your baggage and share some of the ideas and expressions of others that you carry with you as precious merchandise. Anyone may begin. Try to present your valuable cargo with the love which you have for it, reading it or sharing it with the sense in which you treasure it. Share a piece at a time so that everyone gets a chance to participate. You might also follow your presentation with a few words about what the piece that you have shared means to you. Part of the task today is

*learning to listen with reverence—to treasure the treasures of
others even if they are very different from our own values and
tastes. Take your time with this. At the conclusion of your sharing, you might allow each person to state what he or she has
found most valuable in what the others brought to share. Finally,
you might want to copy in your own journal the things you would
like to make a part of your own collection, as well as to enter your
reactions to what we have done together.*

EXCURSIONS IN BRIEF

As you can see, the possibilities for creating journal exercises are infinite, limited only by the imagination of the individuals and groups engaged in writing and sharing. Your own creativity can probably pick up on what we have done so far and shape
other exercises for future work, adapting materials we have already presented in this book and striking out in entirely new
directions. To prompt you a bit more, we have included below a
few more "excursions in brief," strategies for writing that you
might like to experiment with. They are "in brief" not because
they take less time than the exercises you have done previously,
but because the instructions for doing them are presented in short
form. If you have worked with the exercises of "Soul Country"
you will already have a feel for how to go about working with
these strategies and using them in a group and can fill in whatever
is needed for your specific situation. So here they are:

Destinations: A Road Map
Draw a map of places you have intended to go with your life,
personal and career objectives. Show the route you have actually
taken with whatever turns and detours it has involved. Pinpoint
where you are now. Use descriptive language as in the Soul
Country exercise. Explore in your writing your present feelings
about places you went and about places you failed to or chose not
to reach. Are some of these still on your itinerary in some fashion?
Variation: Draw a road map like this, but project it into the

future. What do you expect your destinations to be, your feared obstacles and helpful opportunities? Write about these.

What's In My Name?

Use a whole page of your journal to embellish your given name in whatever way feels good to you. You may make it like an illuminated manuscript, doodle or draw, make connections, associations, write your name in as many ways as you fancy it.

Three Portraits

Use three individuals pages of your journal to draw three portraits of yourself, one each representing the past, present and future. We will title them "I was," "I am" and "I will be." You may use words, symbols, sketches, etc.—whatever appeals to you at the moment to best express each of these stages in your life. Certainly every future could be characterized to some degree or other by the symbol of a question mark and perhaps you want to place one in your future portrait, but, try to go further than that by letting your fantasies, premonitions, and expectations find expression.

In your journal describe your reactions to each of these portraits in detail. What are their connections, dissonances? What mood or feeling does each evoke? What does having them side by side say to you? What times in your life are represented most heavily in your "I was" and your "I will be"? Could you pick different times in your past and future to draw additional portraits of yourself?

How Others See Me

Introduce yourself from the viewpoint of some of the people who are close to you or acquainted with you. How would your spouse, children, parents or other members of your family present you? What would an employer, employee, co-worker, friend, neighbor say? Pick one of these that interests you and write the introduction in your journal just as if it were taking place, live, in a group of people. Imagine seeing yourself through the eyes of the person you have chosen and describe yourself from that perspective as fully as possible.

The Time Machine

Dreams and time machines allow us to travel in another dimension, across the years. Here are a few excursions across the boundaries of time which can enrich your journal writing:

1. What would your younger self say about you today? For example, if you are thirty, what would your eighteen-year-old self be saying if it were present in your life at this moment? What feelings, suggestions, judgements, decisions would your younger self offer you? Try your older self too. Imagine that you are eighty. What would your eighty-year-old self be saying about your life and circumstances if it could look at you now?

2. Imagine a day in your life five or ten years from today. Make it an ideal day, the kind of life you look forward to living. Tell the day just as you see it happening to you from your first waking moment til you fall asleep. Make it graphic and colorful and concrete. You awake. Where are you? Who is with you? What do you wear, eat for breakfast? Tell the story of your work and play.

Journal Journalism

Write some short newspaper articles about highlights of your life up to the present. Try some about things you would like to have happen or accomplish in the future. Cover your marriage, a promotion, your retirement, your funeral.

Create some want ads for some of the things you want in your life. Make them succinct but complete. Do the same for "employment opportunities," listing the requirements for spouse, child, friend, employer, advisor or any other person you would like to have in your life.

Matters of Life and Death

Answer any or all of these questions in your journal. Then expand your answer into a paragraph or a page which expresses what you feel in detail.

Who or what am I willing to live for?

Who or what is killing me?

Who or what do I want to be more alive for?

Who or what am I willing to die for?

The Public Domain and the Private Eye

Make two lists. Let the first one be of your public self, that is of the things that are generally known about you or that you would not be embarrassed to have as common knowledge. In the second, put down the things that you would rather not have known, the things that a private detective would observe. When you've completed these, review them and write about how you feel about them and about any of the specific things that you find on either of the two.

Treaties

What seem to be the agreements, explicit and implicit, which you have with people who are important in your life? Pick a person (perhaps from the exercise on "The Population" of Soul Country) and write out the terms of your treaty with this individual. What do you demand of each other? What are the penalties for failing to keep the terms? Which parts would you like to discuss? Renegotiate? Draw up new or ideal terms for a new treaty from your side.

Social Circles

Draw a series of circles to represent the groups, societies, the collections of people to whom you belong formally and informally, by birth and by choice. Write a paragraph describing how it feels for you to belong to each of these. Which ones overlap? What feelings or conflicts occur for you at these intersections? Describe them.

Instant Replays

Unlike the reruns of football plays on television, our imaginations have the additional capability of seeing things differently from the way we first perceived them. We can change the story, turn tragedy into comedy, and find new outcomes for old stories. Tapping this imagination is one of the ways of releasing energy for change in our lives. When we find ourselves dissatisfied with our own behavior or performance in a specific situation, a rerun may be in order. Take such an event and replay it as you would like to have it happen or would have liked to have seen it take place. Write the replay as you imagine it in your journal.

Finding a Mantra

This is something to do when rereading or reviewing your journal. A mantra is a short saying, phrase or incantation which can be used for meditation or self-suggestion. It can be a reminder of something we tend to forget or the key to an attitude or problem which we want to understand or explore. A few words may capture a very personal mystery. In our journal writing we often create mantra for ourselves far better than any guru can give. So, as you read your journal be on the lookout for the insights, figures of speech which best capture your situation in life, which signal your growth or point to breakthroughs. Here, for example, are a couple which have been useful to me:

Settle in to break out.

There is so much in my life—so live.

The License Bureau

Want to do something new? Something you've been promising yourself for a long time but haven't gotten around to? Something you're just a bit too scared to try? Write yourself a license! Take a page of your journal and use whatever degree of officiousness you find necessary to write yourself a license which permits you to do whatever it is that you've been holding back on. State whatever conditions you require to make it happen, to protect yourself, etc. If you like the outcome, you can always renew the license.

Relics and Memorabilia

Imagine that you have died and a civic committee has been appointed to select some souvenirs from your life, things which you used, wore, possessed, received. What will be found for the display from some of the key points of your life? From this present time? How does each of these mark the period in a special way?

Musical Meandering

Choose a favorite (or an unfamiliar) piece of music. Let your fantasy wander with it and instruct your pen to follow and to record in the journal the imaginings and feelings which result as you discover new places inside of yourself.

The Hidden Sage

There are hidden sources of wisdom living within us. This is a means for tapping them. You may aporoach it in two ways:

1. Relax and concentrate your imagination on some figure who is important to you, one who has been a source of good advice or inspiration in the past, a parent, friend, counselor, a literary or historical figure, perhaps a religious figure like Buddha or Jesus. When you feel that you are very much in touch, when the figure is present to you, allow him or her to speak to you about your life. You may ask questions or even carry on a dialogue. Record what is said or takes place as it happens in your journal.

2. Close your eyes and take a fantasy journey, perhaps to the forest, the mountains, the desert or the sea or to some place that is sacred to you. When you come to a hidden spot on this journey, an advisor or sage will be waiting with wisdom for you. When you encounter this person you will discover who he or she is and can begin to record in your journal what is said. If at any time you feel that you are losing touch with your advisor while writing, close your eyes and re-establish good contact before resuming your writing.

Bank Account

What would an inventory of your check book stubs and credit card receipts tell you about your priorities? Do you seem to be the same person there that you imagine yourself to be? Income tax time might provide an opportunity for viewing your financial, material self and making some notes about it in the journal.

Unfinished Business

The Japanese have a custom of equalizing all debts for the celebration of the New Year. Who are or whom do I imagine to be my debtors and creditors? What is owed? Don't just limit yourself to the dimension of dollars and cents. Is some resolution called for? If so, what steps might bring me closer? Exploring these questions in the journal may bring you nearer to finishing business that is overdue for completion.

Body Mapping

Draw a picture of your body in your birthday suit. Write about how this feels to you. Mark the places on your body where you usually feel energy, excitement, embarrassment, awkwardness or pain. Write about each of these. You may use this sketch as a sort of continuing map of your bodily experiences over a longer period of time. What do your accumulated notes tell you about yourself and the experiences which affect you physically? What consequences do you see and conclusions do you draw? Note these too.

Soul Geneology

Most of us can trace our blood ancestors back at least a generation or two. Some of us can even go back for centuries for our roots. Blue-blooded or red-blooded, each of us has in addition a number of people who have parented us in special ways outside of our familial forebears. These are the people who have inspired, taught, listened, cared for, prayed for, delighted in, or in other ways enriched our lives by being psychological or spiritual parents to us. Some may be real people who were close to us, others distant heroes or heroines or even literary figures. Take a page in your journal and list the folk who could be included in a "soul geneology" of yourself. When you feel that you have satisfactorily noted your spiritual lineage, take as much space as you want to write about and appreciate these persons. You might also do this with the anti-heroes and anti-heroines of your personal story. Letters and dialogues could be used to explore unfinished business that you sense with someone in your past.

Last Will and Testament

Today a last will and testament usually deals only with items of more than ordinary value. (Incidentally, if you don't have a will, the journal is a good place to work out your bequests.) We are charmed, for instance, to read of Will Shakespeare's disposition of a bedstead. Using your journal to make a fantasy will, distributing even your trivia among a host of friends and acquaintances, perhaps even your enemies might be an occasion for exploring the way you value your possessions and the kind of relationship you have with a variety of people. It is a time for feeling, wit, humor, and frankness. Try it.

Advice from Lovers and Others

Who are the two or three people who most truly love me for myself and care about me? What are some of the messages that they continually or consistently give me? Write these down and reflect on them with further writing. These questions may help.

Is there more truth there than I am willing to admit?

What are my suspicions, fears, thoughts about what they are saying or doing?

How do I usually respond?

What other responses are possible?

Do the same with some of the people who feel negative toward you or whom you see in some way critical of or opposed to you.

Lifestyle Image

What are the images that suggest themselves to you as real descriptions of yourself or your lifestyle? Draw or describe one of these images in your journal. Perhaps you see yourself as an unmade bed, or a doormat or a small precious package, an open road or a stop sign—whatever seems right for you. Expand upon it in writing.

Message from Heaven

Imagine that a message from heaven dropped right at your feet. You stop and pick it up. To whom is it addressed? What does it say? What do you do with/about it? Use your journal to write about this.

Freed-up

You have just swallowed a pill that erases all morality and inhibitions. It will free you from shyness, embarrassment, outer constraints and inner censors, and its effect will last for a full week. Set your pen to paper and jot down some of the things that you will do and say during this period. When you have finished, read over your adventures. Are these some things that you feel you might like to try, even without the imaginary pill?

The Book of Life

Imagine that your life is a book. How many important chapters would you see it containing up to the present moment? How would you name each of these chapters? Name each one and write a sentence or two or a short paragraph that captures the essence of each. What major events or decisions begin each chapter or bring it to a close? Do this for the present chapter, too. What future chapters do you imagine? Name these and describe them.

The Turning Wheel

Imagine your life as a wheel. On a page of your journal draw a circle to represent it and at the very center a point or hub to represent yourself. When a wheel turns, those parts closest to the center move with less velocity than those closer to the rim. What things are closer to the center in your life, more stable, permanent, enduring? What things are more peripheral, moving, changing, in flux? Note these things on your wheel. When you have completed it you will have a picture which may help you to clarify values and facilitate decision making. The wheel can be used over again with specific facets of your life to clarify what is central and what is flexible.

Rags to Riches

Suppose you were suddenly reduced to dire poverty. What things in your possession or life style would you struggle hardest to preserve? Expand on your feelings about these things in your writing.

Suppose again that you fell heir to a fabulous fortune. What would you do first? Write about this.

Finally, play God. What would you change or create to make the best possible of all worlds? Describe this process in your journal.

When you have finished one or all of these brief excursions, note any things which suggest themselves as possible changes in your life style right now.

Topper
Devotees of late night television may recall the Topper films. Man, wife and dog, killed in an automobile accident move about the earth as disembodied spirits working benevolent, humorous mischief. What would you do if you were suddenly enabled to move about your world in an invisible form for a few days? Let your fantasy loose and follow its adventure with your pen.

Self-Imaging
Here is a way to use the journal for a bit of creative daydreaming. It seems that forming attractive images of ourselves releases the energies which bring us along in the direction of our imagining. This can often mean an increase of self-confidence, strength and healing. The trick is to allow yourself to see yourself in the mind's eye doing what it is you wish to do or appearing as you wish to appear. Allow yourself the fantasy right down to the bodily feelings that go with it. Record this image as best you can in your journal. A couple of examples might help.

You are anxious about meeting another person—imagine yourself there pulling it off perfectly.

You are down in the dumps—imagine what it is to be really on top of the world.

You are going to run a race—imagine and feel yourself in perfect stride, winning.

Facing My Accusers
What others think of us or what we think others think of us can create quite a block to our energies and prevent us from following our solid instincts. This strategy is a way of dealing with an excess of sensitivity to others' opinions of us or our assumptions about what these opinions might be.

Allow yourself some moments of paranoia in which to make a list of the things you hear people saying about you or fear they could. Write the accusations one after another down one side of a journal page. Then, when you have finished, move to the other side of the page and allow yourself a fearless gut response to each accusing statement. Give the contrary evidence or interpretation that you feel to be true, or tell your accusers to "get lost" if that feels right. Read over your work and note any change of attitude which you feel toward specific situations.

The Daily Mandala

Some people prefer to sum up the day in pictures or symbols before writing in detail. Those who tend to write only about "facts" and fail to record feelings may find this approach helpful. A person can simply draw the image which "feels" right for the day, its parts or the events and encounters it contained. One particularly effective way of doing this is the creation of a mandala for the day. Many variations of this are possible, but the one I like most for journal work is made by drawing a large circle on a full page of the book. Imagining that this is the face of a twenty-four hour clock with twenty-four (midnight) at the nadir and twelve (noon) at the zenith, I can then use pie-shaped fractions of the day to contain the symbols or drawings which best express the content of these hours.

FURTHER RESOURCES FOR JOURNAL KEEPING

Beyond this book, there are a number of places to look for help with journal keeping. First we'll look at several other direct approaches to the journal process and then point out some resources which though not primarily created for journal keeping offer suggestions and techniques which can be easily co-opted into your personal writing.

1. **Ira Progoff:** *Sincere examination of the individual human life is one of man's fundamental religious acts.*

No one has done more to develop and further journal keeping as a method for personal growth than Ira Progoff. He presents his work as a process valid in its own right, accessory to but not competing with religious beliefs and other techniques of spiritual growth and learning. Progoff teaches individuals to look at their lives beginning with the dominant image of the life period in which the individual self is presently found and the contents of that image. They then identify a series of stepping-stones which they consider to be the critical points leading to the present, junctures where certain roads were chosen and others not taken. With each person, event, work and dream in life as well as with one's own body and with society it is possible to create a dialogue, to speak to it and have it speak to us. Much of this work, including what Progoff describes as process meditation, is done in a state of "twilight imaging," a relaxed state of consciousness between waking and sleeping deliberately entered into for the sake of allowing the unconscious to flow freely into awareness, to be perceived and recorded. This process, once learned and practiced in a workshop, can continue as the individual continues his/her own daily log and continues to employ the intensive journal technique.

Progoff's process avoids guided imagery and, despite the fact that journal workshops take place with participants reading aloud in large groups, is non-interactive. The presence of others contains a supportive dynamic, but it is the individual's journal work which provides its own feedback.

Despite the publication of his latest work, Progoff's method must still largely rely on the workshop format for its introduction. Progoff himself and leaders he has trained keep a regular schedule of such workshops at various centers throughout the country. Like all contemplative endeavors, it takes time. It seems to be useful in its existing form for teenagers and adults without respect to cultural or educational background or socioeconomic level. It is costly, but often some scholarship aid is available. The method is open to whatever content the user finds it important to consider, particularly with the dialogue method. In its pure form, what Progoff has developed is not per se a pedagogical tool because of its essentially non-directive nature. Those who use it, however, will find it an adjunct to any form of learning which is capable of dealing with the meaning and value of that learning for the individual's life history.

Information about Ira Progoff's workshops and publications

can be had by writing to Dialogue House Associates, Inc., 45 West Tenth Street, New York, N. Y. 10011.

2. **Milt Hughes:** *You learn to deal with suffering and temptation, and to see God's purpose for everything that happens in your life.*

At the other end of the spectrum lies Milt Hughes' *Spiritual Journey Notebook.* Its subtitle is accurately descriptive, "A Guide for Personal Spiritual Growth Through Developing Basic Disciplines and Specific Actions in the Christian Life." This workbook is explicitly Christian and very directive in that it is based on very clear assumptions about learning and living and witnessing.

Each week begins with making an agenda and a calendar including Bible and other study goals, scripture to memorize and plans for giving personal witness. Special pages facilitate study of the Bible and other books and presentations, prayer concerns and strategies for indepth ministry to others. A spiritual journey section makes space for "a personal account of the day's thoughts, experiences and relationships, of sharing and receiving."

The process is designed for individuals, but group sharing is encouraged. It seems to be useful for both teenagers and older adults. Its simple arrangement and clear instructions would make it immediately comprehensible to almost everyone. The evangelistic flavor of the notebook will recommend it to some and deter others from its use. It is catechetical in the sense that it provides direct incentive to do Bible and other religious reading and study and a method for distilling essential data and keeping it accessible to memory. Some of these techniques could be borrowed for use in classes and study groups.

Milt Hughes' book costs $5.50 and is available from National Student Ministries, 127 Ninth Avenue North, Nashville, Tennessee 37234.

3. **Roberto Assagioli:** *In writing, one expresses different sides of the personality.*

Psychosynthesis is the name given to a process of personal growth and to the movement which fosters it. The basic insights and shape of this movement derive from the thought and leadership of the Italian psychiatrist Roberto Assagioli. The movement presently maintains a center in San Francisco, California, and publishes a journal, *Synthesis*. Psychosynthesis is seen by its proponents as "the conscious attempt to *cooperate* with the natural process of personal development," the "drive in living matter to perfect itself" which in humans becomes a conscious urge toward growth. The working structure of the movement is derived from many traditions and disciplines. Journal keeping is one of these. *Synthesis* in each issue contains a workbook in which the individual finds explicit exercises and explanations of psychosynthesis which can be used in his/her own synthesis of the sub-personalities which are a part of the individual experience of the self. Much of this work is done in writing or drawing and the journal is an important tool for collecting the work as well as recording the flow of daily experience.

Psychosynthesis is a growth discipline of the highest order which uses the journal as a tool within the framework of the principles of human development which it espouses. It is the constellation of these principles which gives shape to the journal exercises. Many people who have been turned off to the human potential movement because of what they see to be its excesses will be encouraged by this philosophy which makes as much of the will and the rational sides of the human personality as it does of the emotive and the organic.

Programs in psychosynthesis are held at The Psychosynthesis Institute, 3352 Sacramento Street, San Francisco, California 94118, and The Canadian Institute of Psychosynthesis, 3496 Avenue Marlowe, Montreal, Quebec H4A 3L7.

4. **Christina Baldwin:** *The journal is a river . . . is a mirror . . . is an anchor . . . is myself . . . The journal is a process of survival.*

One to One: Self Understanding through Journal Writing by Christina Baldwin is an excellent approach to the journal process. Some of the bones of the Progoff method appear to support the structure, but Ms. Baldwin has covered them handsomely with borrowings from Gestalt, transactional analysis and, most important, from her own rich experiences with her journal, from which she quotes freely. The book promises to be helpful to many journal writers, especially women—the author is a feminist who writes with women in mind, but without excluding or depreciating men. The literary quality of her own writing is outstanding and even somewhat intimidating to those of us who write more prosaically, yet this is just another demonstration of the potential of the journal to play midwife to the talents and skills of those who use it. Ms. Baldwin gives workshops in journal writing throughout the country and may be reached through Henry Morrison, Inc., 58 West 10th Street, New York, N.Y. 10011.

The Values Clarification Movement

The Values Clarification Movement is a humanistic trend in education which seeks to support the student's personal growth in values by accentuating the worth and capability of the learner. The name most prominently associated with this work is that of Dr. Sidney B. Simon of the School of Education of the University of Massachusetts at Amherst. His numerous publications and lecture tours have enriched teachers and through them students throughout the country.

The techniques of values clarification are strongly oriented toward consulting the person and values of the learner. For this reason, although most of the materials have been created for primary and secondary school situations, grown-ups find them exciting and provocative. They are a ready resource for journal keeping strategies which adult individuals and groups can pursue in greater depth than children.

Four of my favorite books in this field which have great applicability to journal keeping are:

Hawley, Simon and Britton, *Composition For Personal Growth*, New York, Hart Publishing Company, 1973.

Hall, Brian, *Values Clarification as Learning Process* (*Guidebook* and *Sourcebook*), Ramsey, N.J., Paulist Press, 1974.

Canfield and Wells, *100 Ways to Enhance Self-Concept in the Classroom*, Englewood Cliffs, N.J., Prentice-Hall, Inc., 1976.

Simon, Howe and Kirschenbaum, *Values Clarification: A Handbook of Practical Strategies For Teachers and Students*

Career Development

Another source for ways to explore one's life through writing has emerged from the activities of placement counselors and employment consultants. Knowing one's self is a vital prelude to making career decisions and job choices. Counselors in these fields have consequently developed and adopted a variety of strategies for this. Many of the techniques employ imaginative perspectives for writing about one's preferences and tastes and personal resources. Two books which contain these methods in abundance are:

Bolles, Richard, *What Color is Your Parachute?*, Berkeley, California, Ten Speed Press, 1972.

Crystal, John and Bolles, Richard, *Where Do I Go From Here With My Life?*, New York, Seabury Press, 1974.

Some useful suggestions can be found in:

Lakein, Alan, *How To Get Control of Your Time and Your Life*, New York, Peter H. Widen, Inc., 1973.

The Church of the Latter Day Saints

Perhaps no other group of people in America has had a more consistent concern with geneology and personal life history than the Mormon Church. Prophet Joseph Smith advised the members of the Church at its inception to keep careful records of experiences, decisions and learnings. This counsel is important even to the present day for many members of the church. The journal is a *sine qua non* for recording the missionary experiences of each young Mormon who sets out to do this work. This church's propensity for record keeping has contributed to making its geneological library one of the finest in the world.

Mormon bookstores generally contain a good selection of blank books for journals and diaries, along with advice about how to search out geneologies and create personal records. One brief and simple but attractive paperback by J. Malan Heslop and Dell Van Orden is entitled *How to Write Your Personal History* (Salt Lake City, 1976, Bookcraft Inc.) This book can be particularly useful for those who consider the assembling of a personal biography to be an important part of their journal work. Some who are not a part of the Church of the Latter-Day Saints could be uncomfortable with the religious flavor of certain examples quoted in the book. Nonetheless it does give a solid set of hints and suggestions about the sources and methods of writing one's own story, even if handing down this story to others is not a primary concern as it is in the Morman community.

NOTES

1. Helen Rezatto, "My Diary," *St. Anthony Messenger*, July, 1971, p. 31.
2. Sheldon B. Kopp, *If You Meet the Buddha on the Road, Kill Him!* (Palo Alto, California: Science and Behavior Books) 1972, p. 4.
3. Graham Greene, *A Sort of Life* (New York: Pocket Books) 1974, p. 9–10.
4. Merle Shane, *Some Men Are More Perfect Than Others* (New York: Bantam Books) 1974, p. 119.
5. Mary Jane Moffit and Charlotte Painter, eds., *Revelations: Diaries of Women* (New York: Random House) 1974, p. 5.
6. Patricia Hampl, "A Book with a Lock and Key," *The Lamp in the Spine*, No. 9, Spring-Fall, 1974, p. 51–52.
7. *Ibid.*, p. 50.
8. Gordon Tappan, "Notes on Journal Keeping." Unpublished note circulated by the Psychology Department of Sonoma State College, p. 3.
9. George F. Simons, *Journal for Life I: Foundations* and *Journal for Life, II: Theology from Experience* (Chicago: ACTA Foundation) 1975 and 1977.
10. Helen Rezatto, *Art. Cit.*, p. 32.
11. Jo Fleming, *His Affair* (New York: M. Evans & Co.) 1976, p. 182.
12. *Ibid.*, p. 18.
13. Frank Potter, in *Spiritual Journeys*, November, 1976, p. 2.
14. Ann Faraday, *Dream Power* and *The Dream Game* (New York: Harper & Row) 1973 and 1974.
15. Kathleen Cox, "A Journal of the Unconscious," *The Lamp in the Spine*, No. 9, Spring-Fall, 1974, p. 58–59.
16. Norman Brown in *Glamour*, September, 1975, p. 92.
17. Robert U. Akeret, *Photoanalysis* (New York: Pocket Books) 1975, p. 35–36.
18. Gordon Tappan, *Art. Cit.*, p. 4–8.
19. *Ibid.*, p. 2.
20. From an unpublished piece by Marilyn Lang, instructor in oral communications at Humbolt State College, Arcata, California.
21. Helen Rezatto, *Art. Cit.*, p. 33.

22. Abraham Maslow, *The Farther Reaches of Human Nature* (New York: Viking Press) 1971, p. 36.

23. Address to the 1975 annual meeting of the Association for Humanistic Psychology, Estes Park, Colorado.

24. Abraham Maslow, *Op. Cit.*, p. 36–37.